ART NOUVEAU FURNITURE

ART NOUVEAU FURNITURE

Alastair Duncan

228 illustrations 49 in colour

Thames and Hudson

To Caroline

Printed in Japan by Dai Nippon

CONTENTS

Acknowledgments

Gratitude is extended to the numerous people in Europe and the United States who provided ready assistance and advice.

In Brussels, most particularly, to Messrs Meurrens & Weynans for the use of their library; Father J.-G. Watelet; Mr and Mrs Roland Gillion-Crowet; Mrs M. Thery; Mr Chardin; Mr P. Thery; and Mrs Janine Duesberg.
In Paris, to Mr Felix Marcilhac; Mr J.-P. Camard; Mr Robert Walker; Mr Nico Borsjé; Mr J.-C. Brunot; and Miss Andrée Vyncke.
In Nancy, to Mrs F. T. Charpentier; Mrs Natalie Dobransky; and, in Geneva, to Mr G. de Bartha.
In the United States, especially, to Mr Lloyd Macklowe of Macklowe Gallery; Mr Benedict Silverman; Mr William Feldstein, Jr.; Mr Ira Simon; Mr and Mrs John Mecom, Jr.; Mr Robert Sage; Mr Gary Calderwood, and Mr Grady Cain.

In photography, the following are especially to be thanked: Mr David Robinson; Miss Janet Lamson; Mr Laurent Sully Jaulmes; Mr John D. Kisch; Mr J.-L. Charmet; Mr G. Mangin; Mrs Sonia Edard; and Mr Steven Tucker.

INTRODUCTION

Though the movement in the decorative arts that has become known as 'Art Nouveau' emerged in the 1890s, it is best understood by looking back to nearly a hundred years before. For at the beginning of the nineteenth century there was a noticeable lack of imaginative innovation among designers. This was particularly true in the case of furniture: the French, who had predominated in this field for almost a century, seemed to find themselves at the end of a chain-like sequence of distinct styles – Louis XIV, Régence, Louis XV, Louis XVI, Consulat, Directoire, Empire, Restauration. It appeared as if no avenue had been left unexplored, no legitimate structural form or decorative theme untried. In this impasse, designers in the 1820s took to rehashing past modes, either by slavish reproduction of the masterpieces of the great and original eighteenth-century *ébenistes* or by undiscriminating borrowing of various elements from each of the preceding periods. The result was a leaning towards curious hybrids, such as Louis XIV Boulle commodes on tapering cylindrical Louis XVI feet enhanced with Louis XV ormolu *sabots*. By the time of Napoleon III (1852), this hotchpotch, which was referred to in France as 'all the Louis', prevailed to the point where art historians and critics railed at the patent lack of creativity. This became particularly evident at the 1867 Exposition Universelle in Paris; the director of the International Jury, Michel Chevalier, wrote with a note of grief about the eclectic items on exhibition, 'from the surviving monuments of our art, future historians will take us to be a fantastic people, living partially in the Greek tradition, partly in that of the Italian Renaissance, and partly as eighteenth-century Bourbons, but never having had an original life of our own.'

By 1870, when Napoleon III's Second Empire came to its ignominious end, the pastiche of French furniture design was being called 'Le style sans style'. And in Europe as a whole, the situation was largely the same. Only Biedermeier, introduced in Germany and Austria from 1815, provided a brief shining moment of innovation, even though it was a direct and rather obvious neo-classical clone. In England, Victorian furniture was characterized by its fetish for ornamentation. Chairs and desks were adorned by elaborately pierced crest-rails and frieze drawers – often with a strong oriental or Hispano-Moresque influence. Flock wallpapers and colourful damask upholstery added to the congested, if not cluttered, appearance of rooms in most nineteenth-century English homes. In the United States, where English furniture had been the primary source of inspiration for over a hundred years, the New York immigrant cabinetmaker, John Belter, introduced a form of Rococo revivalism: heavily carved and plushly upholstered parlour and bedroom suites most appropriately described in a contemporary article as 'Louisiana bordello'!

Elsewhere on the East Coast the manufacturers Herter Brothers and Hunzinger produced their own distinctive styles of fundamentally ornate Victorian furniture.

The furniture shown at the 1889 Exposition Universelle in Paris served to underscore the static situation, at least in the eyes of the Jury's director, who wrote, 'This love of the old has taken on such proportions that when an artist makes an original work he is immediately criticized and judged very severely if it does not appear, at first glance, to adapt itself faithfully to a well-known and readily classified style.'

A M. Picard, appointed by the French government to publish a report on the Exposition, expressed a similar sense of frustration: 'This cult of the past has been pushed to excess. It absorbs all intelligence, all science, and all the efforts of the heads of establishments and designers who confine themselves to copying and restoration. A piece of furniture which does not adapt itself easily to such or such a class is immediately the object of the most virulent criticism. The adventurous who have deviated are branded as either ignorant or sacrilegious. One sees only Henri II, Louis XIV, XV, or XVI. New ideas are proscribed.'

But as always in aesthetic development, there were contradictory voices to be heard outside the establishment and mainstream. Imaginative spirits here and there were searching for a new beginning, a new door to open, and in many cases it was the theorists who led the way. Viollet-le-Duc's *Entretiens sur l'Architecture*, published between 1863 and 1872, became the academic lodestar by which Hector Guimard, Victor Horta, and many others justified their architecture forty years later. Likewise, the writings of Ruskin and Morris were found to contain the seeds of Art Nouveau's birth and growth. Later, Eugène Grasset's *Principes de Composition Décorative* translated and updated these to meet the late nineteenth-century's creative needs. Within five short years independent designers in England, Belgium, and France had forged a revolutionary international movement, one which called for the unification of *all* aspects of design, whether buildings, furnishings, fashion, or jewelry. Architects provided the early impetus. Convention was turned on its head; not only were whiplash organic contours introduced on to the façades of buildings, but entire interiors were designed to match. Interior decorators and artists picked up where the architects left off. Disciples flocked to the style as new magazines and exhibitions provided a cross-fertilization of ideas.

None, perhaps, caught the prevailing mood of cooperation and optimism among the promoters of the new style more clearly than the art critic Francis Jourdain. In an 1899 article on modern furniture in *La Revue d'Art*, he wrote, 'It is a time when the architect walks hand-in-hand with the artist, sculptor, engraver, musician, man-of-letters, and the decorator. All have an identical vision, a common aesthetic goal, and a single ideal in which, without forfeiting any of their own personalities, they can together create harmony [which is] ... so subtle, indefinable and vague, and yet so clear, that it can be called a style ...'

Various experiments undertaken in isolation gradually coalesced until the Art Nouveau style, which took its inspiration from Nature and substituted sinuous, natural curves for the more conventional and familiar shapes of traditional design, evolved in the late 1890s into a *bona fide* movement, one which, however, not surprisingly suffered growing pains. The critics – the same ones who had for so long been admonishing the decorative arts to slough off the mistakes of the past – were quick to find fault. Few styles, indeed, have received so much censure so promptly or so vehemently. The Art Nouveau exponent must have felt both confused and betrayed. A typical early criticism was that of Verneuil, the editor of *Art et Décoration*, who wrote in 1897, 'It is regrettable that no one can break with the past. Now there exists either a salad of styles or the "Modern Style", an invention to which madness the Salon des Incohérents have opened their doors with joy. . . . whose products are to be found here and there with their menacing tentacles, ready to seize the imprudent who approaches. We are turning in a vicious circle. The large percentage of the public does not want to change from the old styles because, beyond these, there is nothing good. Most furniture-makers therefore refuse to experiment with new designs because the public won't change. . . . And everyone is right.'

In 1900 the critic G. M. Jacques wrote in *L'Art Décoratif* of Art Nouveau's 'Reign of Terror', although the movement was then barely ten years old. To be precise, it was Art Nouveau furniture, more than any other category, which angered the Parisian critics. Glass and jewelry, for example, were considered suitable for the depiction of flowers and insects; neither had a great French tradition to uphold, nor was either considered a major applied art form. It was safe to find the vases of Emile Gallé pleasing; there was no precedence by which they could, or should, be judged. Even those appalling *femme-fleur* electric lamps, in which draped bronze Belle Epoque nymphs held aloft electric bulbs cunningly designed as flower sprays, were seen as harmless early attempts to harness the new Fairy Electricity. In furniture, however, no such latitude was permissible: the magnificent heritage of France's eighteenth-century cabinetmakers – and monarchs! – was at stake.

The fundamental problem with Art Nouveau furniture was that it violated the basic laws of cabinetmaking: a piece of furniture had above all to be well-constructed and functional; only then did one set about decorating it. Turn-of-the-century designers, however, in their rush to recreate Nature, put the emphasis on the decoration. At its epogee, an Art Nouveau piece of furniture resembled a flowering bush or tree: its feet were transformed into roots; its framework into the trunk and main branches; and its cornice into blossoms. If this was not bad enough, various entomological horrors – beetles, dragon-flies, and bugs – became bronze drawer pulls or random sculpted decoration. Purists cried out loudly at the style's worst excesses, ignoring the quieter masterpieces by Louis Majorelle of Nancy, Eugène Gaillard of Paris, Victor Horta of Brussels and many others which fell well within traditional limits.

Gallé, whose glasswork had proved so popular, was a frequent transgressor when it came to furniture. An article in *Le Figaro* in 1898 discussed his newly-created dragonfly table: 'a fluttering dragonfly, immobilized for an instant, has lent its wings to the proportions of a console – witness the Gallé table supported by three dragonfly bodies. The enlargement of the frail insects to the dimensions of a table leg has transformed them into monstrous creatures. This disregard for scale is a grave error . . .'

Also attacked were Art Nouveau's favourite motifs themselves: Lorraine umbels (cow parsley) and poppies simply did not match the grandeur of the formal acanthus or anthemion sprays of yesteryear. Nor could a floral or land-scape marquetry panel be as majestic as a vase of summer flowers on a *sans traverse* lattice-work or parquetry ground.

Not all commentary, of course, was negative, nor was it aimed at all Art Nouveau designers. The same critic who had written a year earlier of the reign of terror, found Georges de Feure's furniture at the 1900 Exposition Universelle delightful. He wrote, 'de Feure's exhibit characterizes perfectly the spirit of Bing's shop. It is not the work of a revolutionary; it is not a question of over-throwing everything or of turning everything upside down, of exterminating the legitimate past and of eliminating the rules of geometry. It is, to the con-trary, a true return to nature of which the first innovators, hot-headed in their impetuosity to destroy, had lost their vision. Each piece of de Feure's furniture is, above all, a good, honest, and unpretentious work of cabinetry.'

Others rallied to the cause. In Paris, for example, Samuel Bing and Julius Meier-Graefe, both of whom opened Art Nouveau galleries, were ardent publicists of the style which they had helped to launch, while certain critics – in particular Gustave Soulier – promoted Art Nouveau in their coverage of the annual Salons. In his hometown Nancy, Gallé generated an endless litany of written and spoken words to promote Nature's cause. Other enthusiasts were the Goncourt brothers, Roger Marx and Emile Nicolas, all noted art critics born in Lorraine. In the rest of Europe, comment was more restrained. The foreign critics who covered the Paris Salons and international expositions – expecially those in *The Studio* and *Deutsche Kunst und Dekoration* – spent more time bemoaning their own countrymen's inabilities than finding fault elsewhere.

The Art Nouveau era brought the concept of the *ensemblier* to maturity. Prior to 1900 pieces of furniture were often designed individually, each to fit willy-nilly into the general disharmony of a mid-nineteenth-century home. Whereas seat furniture tended to be *en suite*, one had to search separately for the tables, plant stands, and vitrines that completed the drawing-room. No common theme unified an interior: period rooms in the Bethnal Green Museum, London, and the Metropolitan Museum of Art, New York, show that eclecticism was the norm. The Art Nouveau philosophy of integrated design brought a decided change; a room had to be planned in its entirety, and furniture designers were forced to show much greater diversity. One curiosity of the period was a seeming fall from favour of two eighteenth-century pieces of furniture: the commode and *bonheur-du-jour*, a lady's desk or work-table. Both were absent from the repertoire of most turn-of-the-century cabinetmakers and both regained their former splendour in the 1920s. The reason for this is uncertain. The commode appears to have lost ground to two larger pieces, the *armoire* and *meuble d'appui*, as a storage facility, while the *bonheur-de-jour* was superseded by the slightly smaller lady's desk. The *bureau plat*, another eighteenth-century masterpiece of French furniture, also largely disappeared.

By 1905 Art Nouveau's impetus was spent. The public soon tired of the legions of bronze sirens and bugs which pervaded the Salons. The brilliance of the *fin-de-siècle* dimmed, and life returned to its humdrum normality. In furniture, veneered flora and fauna were suddenly back where they belonged – in the Lorraine countryside. Europe's bourgeoisie had suffered a fall in its standard of living as populations swelled; less disposable income for the average home owner required a range of cheaper mass-produced furnishings, a challenge immediately met by designers in Germany, Austria and the Low Countries. French cabinetmakers reacted reluctantly to the prospect of lowered standards, allowing their northern neighbours to make inroads into the domestic market. In late 1902, the Chambre Syndicate de l'Ameublement staged its first Salon des Industries du Mobilier at the Grand-Palais in Paris. The aim was threefold: to boost the local furniture industry in the faubourg Saint-Antoine; to change French taste; and to combat the progress made by the foreign furniture retailers in Paris. Incorporated into the Salon was a competition for cheap furniture in which French manufacturers were invited to participate. Many Art Nouveau designers responded, among them Mathieu Gallerey, Georges de Feure, Henri Rapin, and Théodore Lambert. Gone were the lavish mouldings and sculpted decoration of five years earlier; in their place were lightly carved floral panels on rectangular frames. The emphasis had shifted. Economy was the new watchword, one which some critics felt went unheeded. As René Blum wrote in his review of the third Salon in 1908: 'For a piece of furniture to be sold cheaply it must be reproduced in a large edition. The close collaboration of artist, manufacturer, and retailer therefore seems indispensable. I firmly believe that it is because of the absence of such collaboration that most of the tentative efforts in the last years have failed.'

This period of austerity ushered in the range of furniture now described as 'transitional'. It saw the eclipse of most Art Nouveau designers; by the outbreak of World War I almost all had ceased their participation in the Salons. Contemporary periodicals show a range of rational, yet uninspired *ensembles* which, everyone agreed, precisely met the needs of the times. From a decorative standpoint, however, they were unspeakably dull.

It is one of the curiosities in the short history of Art Nouveau that whereas American artists and craftsmen made a significant contribution to the movement in various other fields – particularly glassware, lamps and ceramics – Art Nouveau furniture as such never caught on at all in the United States, and therefore there are no American examples in this book.

It was in the 1920s that Art Nouveau furniture was first seriously reassessed. The characteristics of the new epoch became simplicity of line, richness of material, and sobriety of decoration. Beauty demanded the perfect adaptation of an object to its use. Art Deco proponents, exhilarated by what they considered a return to rationalism, were relentless. The two styles were, of course, antithetical, so little quarter was given when their respective virtues and faults were analysed. Francis Jourdain showed how far his earlier sympathies for Art Nouveau had eroded when he wrote in 1920, 'It is more and more apparent that simplicity is not synonymous with poverty and that civilization, if it has other needs than barbarism, has also different aptitudes. It is more sensitive to the beauty of proportion, harmony of surface, volume and line, and more offended by obvious and exterior ornamentation. It appeals to the intelligence.'

In the new decade superfluous decoration was banished; form would follow function. The Austrian architect Adolf Loos's pre-War caveat was recalled, 'ornament = crime'. Art Nouveau furniture received perhaps its harshest criticism in a 1920 article in *The Studio*: 'Furniture has an architecture of its own, of which the principles have been gradually evolved down the centuries. These laws cannot be disregarded except at risk of the gravest mistakes, the chief of which is to make a piece of furniture the fantasy of the hour, and not a lasting thing; tempting its owner, a few years later, to banish it to an attic corner as something intolerable.'

Sixty years later one can give a more dispassionate assessment. Was Art Nouveau furniture a stylistic detour, or even a *cul-de-sac*, in the history of world furniture? Did it, unlike the glorious glass, jewelry, and ceramics of the period, violate the fundamental laws which governed its medium? There is no simple answer. The concept of Art Nouveau was interpreted in so many ways in so many countries that no common denominator can be applied. There is no similarity between Josef Hoffmann's *Fledermaus* chair, which in its spartan form anticipated the Bauhaus and Modern Style, and the outrageous musical seaweed ensemble which André Metthey and Albert Tassu designed for Pleyel, Wolff and Lyon at the Exposition Universelle, beyond their search for a new beginning. Likewise, the furniture of Henry van de Velde, Charles Rennie Mackintosh, and Josef Olbrich has never been so controversial (either at the time or later) as that of the French. Yet it, too, was revolutionary in its search for a radical break with the past. One cannot, therefore, judge all Art Nouveau furniture designers by a common set of rules. Each had a different interpretation of modernism; furniture took as many forms as there were concepts. Certainly the fundamentals of common sense and good taste were broken by several of the French in their exuberant embrace of the new style, but there were many more who never transgressed, as even a cursory glance through these pages will show. The style's most celebrated cabinetmakers, in fact, take their place among history's finest.

3

4

6

7

9

10

11

12

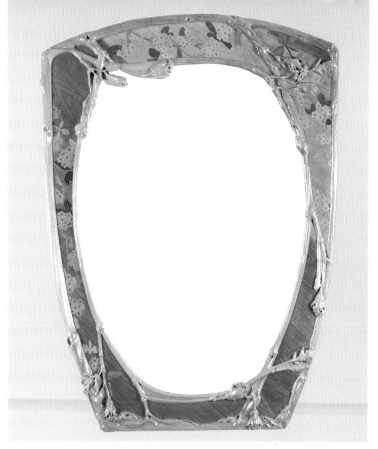

13

14

WOODS
MARQUETRY
MOUNTS

Woods

As in any era, turn-of-the-century furniture-makers had their preferred woods. Mahogany ruled supreme. Its dark grain, buffed and varnished repeatedly until it acquired a rich chocolate-brown hue, imparted a feeling of sumptuosity and wealth. Other popular dark woods were walnut and rosewood, while a wide range of paler species, some exotic, were preferred by Guimard and Gallé: pear, teak, ash, maple, and *jarrah*.

Victor Champier, in his 1910 article on wood in *Art et Industrie*, highlighted a most interesting, and most certainly overlooked, feature of Art Nouveau furniture: 'due to the exaggerated curves and contortions inherent in the movement's style, its furniture needed a set of structural rules different to those normally followed. These curves necessitate extra preparation to retain the wood's strength and solidity. If this furniture had been made in the eighteenth century, the wood would have been conditioned accordingly – largely with fire – to allow such free shapes. Our artisans carve their curves into blocks of wood, severing or cutting across the fibres. The material's mass should be tripled to offset this. The material is given a shape rather than shape given to the material.'

Champier's point was well made. One must agree, as one examines the illustrations in this book, that some Art Nouveau furniture designers showed scant respect for, or awareness of, the wood's ability to meet its functional needs. Certain chairs, in particular, have intricately pierced and carved flower-form splats and sinewy legs that, if sat on, simply beg destruction. They would better have been made in metal or bronze.

Marquetry

By tradition a French form of furniture decoration, marquetry remained in fashion at the turn of the century. In Paris, however, it was limited almost entirely to the reproduction of Louis XV and XVI furniture by industrial *ébénistes* such as Beurdeley, Sormani, Dasson, Durand, and Linke. Their veneers were those of the eighteenth-century masters whose work they copied: kingwood, satinwood, and thuya. Few Art Nouveau furniture designers in Paris were similarly persuaded of the need for marquetry. Certain pieces by

Charpentier and Hérold became the exceptions that confirmed the rule – Parisians preferred sculpted bas-reliefs and serpentine moulded curves as decoration.

It was in Nancy that marquetry was most ardently espoused; hardly a piece of furniture from the ateliers of Gallé, Gauthier, Hestaux and a host of now unidentifiable lesser cabinet shops did not include a perfunctory central panel inlaid with flora or *tableaux* of the Lorraine countryside. More ambitious pieces were covered inside and out with vignettes of glorious Nature: insects, palm fronds and streams meandering from far-off mountain peaks. The critics were cautious; though most of them lauded this latest chapter in the proud tradition of French marquetry, they found the theme of Nature incompatible with the furniture's future setting. Landscapes and flowers were visually too busy, and, to be quite honest, not really dignified. They clashed with the harmony of the average French home. Much preferred were the cube parquetry and trellis-work patterns of earlier styles. Still, there was no denying the Nanceians' cabinetry expertise: the marquetry was faultlessly executed. The subtle gradations of colour and tonal nuances of the woods chosen were beyond reproach, as was the judicious introduction of metal, mother-of-pearl, tortoise shell, horn, and ivory inlays to provide emphasis.

Today it is extremely difficult to identify with certainty the veneers used in Art Nouveau furniture. Seventy-five years of wear and dirt have combined to form an effective disguise. In addition, many veneers were branded or stained with animal or vegetable dyes to add definition and colour to the original composition (Gallé, in particular, used a large number of stained woods). These further complicate identification. Fortunately, an 1898 article in *Art et Décoration* by Edmé Couty, himself a marqueteur, identified the veneers most popular with contemporary furniture makers, including Majorelle, Chevrel and Girod. An anonymous article a year later in *La Lorraine Artiste* provides a nearly identical list used in Nancy. Veneers were divided into two categories:

INDIGENOUS:
>   maple, olive, holly, linden, alder, sycamore, apricot, *alizier*, cypress, and oak.

EXOTIC:
>   mahogany, amaranth, amboyna, lemon-tree, palisander, rosewood, sandalwood, and thuya.

In all, over 500 veneers were available to the marqueteur from which to select whatever burled, streaked, spotted or *moiré* effect was desired. Add to this the process of dyeing, and his palette was complete.

Mounts

No Art Nouveau exponent could respectfully claim full adherence to the movement's doctrines without applying himself to the smallest of details: the very keyholes and lock plates of a room's doors and furniture. The decorative motifs that adorned everything else had to repeat themselves even at this level. Gallé and Majorelle both placed sufficient importance on this aspect of their furniture designs to reserve double-page spreads in the School of Nancy's 1903 catalogue to show a wide selection of flowered and insect drawer pulls and hinges. In Paris, also, examples by Sauvage and Charpentier were illustrated in *Art et Décoration* in 1899 and 1900 respectively.

French turn-of-the-century cabinetmakers followed in the grand tradition of their seventeenth- and eighteenth-century predecessors in the preference for bronze mounts over other metals and alloys. Foundry work in 1900 was still comparable in quality to that of a hundred years earlier. The chasing and gilding of Majorelle's water lily capitals and *sabots* match, in both size and splendour, those cast for Cressent by Jacques Caffieri in the 1770s. Likewise the pierced bronze dragonfly galleries and friezes on Gallé's vitrines are *objets d'art* in themselves, crisply carved and richly patinated.

Revived in the late 1800s by Emile Robert after a long period of disuse, wrought-iron became an acceptable alternative to bronze. In fact, the respectability afforded it by, *inter alios*, Majorelle, Rapin, and Bellery-Desfontaines, ushered in the huge popularity it enjoyed in the 1920s when Brandt, Subes and many other metalworkers chose it over other materials for their furniture, electric lamps and architectural fixtures. In the Art Nouveau period wrought-iron was used principally for door hinges, being given a hammered (*martelé*) finish and then painted metallic grey or black, colours which were found to draw out the richness of certain dark woods more effectively than bronze.

Beyond France the emphasis on furniture mounts was less pronounced. Only Horta and Bugatti used them significantly as a decorative fillip; most of the other designers incorporated formal vegetal motifs or C-scrolls into their metal drawer pulls or bail handles.

DESIGNERS

School of Nancy

It had long been Emile Gallé's goal to create an alliance of the industrial arts in Lorraine; his selection of glass and furniture inspired 'by the fauna and flora of our countryside' at the 1889 Exposition Universelle was the seed which finally came to fruition in the foundation of the School of Nancy on 1 July 1901. Gallé was elected President, with Prouvé, Majorelle and Daum as Vice-Presidents.

The school's charter, published in the *Bulletin des Sociétés Artistiques de l'Est*, listed its aims: to create a professional school of instruction for the industrial arts; to found a museum, library, and permanent collection; to organize conferences; to publish a bulletin; and to arrange expositions and competitions. (A typical competition, arranged in 1907 by the Maison des Magasins Réunis, invited entrants to submit designs for a nine-piece suite of dining-room furniture. A first prize of 750 francs was offered.)

As one goes down the list of members, one is astonished that such an abundance of talent could have accumulated in a provincial town at a single moment. In furniture, the principal exponents were Majorelle, Gallé, Gruber, Vallin and, a generation younger, Gauthier, Hestaux, Neiss, and Férez. To all of these the multi-talented and ubiquitous Prouvé gave assistance with designs and technical counsel. A host of other artisans provided ancillary furniture materials: Finot, Bussière, and Wittman (sculpture); Fridrich and Courteix (fabrics and textiles); the Daum brothers (glass); Lombard (leather); the Mougin brothers (ceramics); and Friant (paintings). Other names punctuate the articles on the Nancy School in contemporary art reviews: Gutton, Déon, Munier, Horel, and the architects André and Weissenburger.

Art Nouveau furniture produced in Nancy has one main characteristic: the use of nature – and most specifically the flower and its components – as the central decorative theme, either as sculpted supports and mouldings or as marquetry floral or landscape panels. Nowhere else was such a realistic interpretation placed on nature. In Paris, the plant was stylized and refined; in Germany and Austria its influence was further removed, if not absent.

Gallé's success in 1889 became the catalyst for the 'new' style. Disciples quickly emerged to exhibit alongside him at both local exhibitions and Paris Salons. By 1900 this loosely-knit group of artisans presented a united front to the outside world. The School's 1903 and 1904 expositions in Paris and Nancy brought full recognition and international fame.

16

19

20

22

23

24

Emile André

André was a prominent Nanceian architect known primarily for his housing project at Saurupt Park. Other of his commissions to receive publicity were a country house for M. Huot and a distinctly Art Moderne structure with serpentine contours and wrought-iron grillwork for M. Lejeune on the boulevard Lobeau, very similar to the house which Louis Majorelle built for himself on the rue Vieux-Aître. André's desire to design the furniture for these houses led him into association with Eugène Vallin and, thereby, into participating in the Ecole de Nancy's expositions.

At the Pavillon de Marsan in Paris, in 1903, his exhibit included a range of furniture in ebony and mahogany. Included were a stool carved with seaweed, a four-leaf screen inlaid with chestnut branches, and a *guéridon* with umbels. He later collaborated separately with the architects Henri Gutton and Georges Munier to design furniture marketed through the retailer, François Vaxelaire et Cie. His style was restrained by Nancy standards: tall, elegant plant stands have lightly carved fluting or leafage similar to, but less pronounced than, those of Vallin; stools have straight stretchers with pierced tenons beneath cushioned floral seats; a triptych screen is enhanced with inlaid hortensia blossoms.

Most critics admired the sobriety and logic of André's designs. Some found them too rectilinear, lacking the organic whimsy that was seemingly *de rigueur* in the work of any Lorraine cabinetmaker.

Férez

Férez was one of the younger generation of cabinetmakers in the Ecole de Nancy. His lengthy apprenticeship was served as a collaborator with Gruber and, to a lesser extent, with Vallin. He emerged as an accomplished wood sculptor and marqueteur in his own right, one whose workmanship finally rivalled those of his erstwhile masters. Among his major works was a series of *armoires* inlaid with medicinal plants commissioned by a Nancy pharmacy. At the 1903 exposition of the Ecole de Nancy at the Pavillon de Marsan in Paris, Férez displayed a bedroom for a young girl which the critic Emile Nicolas described as 'of an agreeable simplicity'; the following year his entry at the Exposition of the Société Lorraine des Amis des Arts included a bureau-bookcase.

Emile Gallé

Gallé brought the same Art Nouveau philosophies to his furniture that he did to everything else. A lengthy, if not tendentious, treatise entitled 'Contemporary Furniture decorated from Nature' was published in three parts in *La Lorraine Artiste* in 1900 and 1901. In it Gallé defined his thoughts, beginning with a summary of the earlier nineteenth-century pastiche of styles which the present 'renaissance' had rejected. The function of every type of furniture was then examined in relationship to the style of decoration to which it was best suited. Then each part – support, leg, bracket, etc. – was studied separately to determine its relative importance to the whole. Finally, Gallé discussed the merits of various cabinetmaking techniques.

In the same way, Gallé applied botanical and entomological motifs to his furniture exactly as he did to his glass and faience. Nature ruled supreme. Readings of Godron's *Flore Française* and *Flore Lorraine* as a student at the Lycée had ignited Gallé's interest in the flora and fauna of his native Lorraine. Periwinkles, wild cherries, convolvuli, gentians, maples, vines, lianas, eglantines, buttercups, were only a few of the flowers which he exploited in the pursuit of beauty. Some, such as the thistle (Lorraine's official emblem), umbel, clematis, and orchid, became perennial favourites. Insects and creatures of the night likewise proliferated; dragonflies, bats, butterflies and snails hovered, flew and crawled over virtually everything.

The writings of the period's foremost men-of-letters were borrowed to endorse nature's cause. Victor Hugo, Maurice Maeterlinck, Théophile Gautier, Théodore de Bonville, and many more, were quoted; their poems, verses, and couplets were branded or veneered into table tops and *armoires*. Many of these were listed in contemporary regional journals such as *Le Bulletin de la Société d'horticulture de Nancy* and *La Gazette des Beaux-Arts*. The following verse by Baudelaire was given as the one which most closely represented Gallé's philosophy:

> *La Nature est un temple – où de vivants piliers*
> *Laissent parfois sortir de confuses paroles.*
> *L'homme passe à travers des forêts de symboles*
> *Qui l'observent avec des regards familiers.*

Gallé's preoccupation with nature extended even to the bronze mounts on his furniture: the catalogue for the School of Nancy's 1903 exposition lists insects and flowers by function:

BRONZE FURNITURE MOUNTS:

Drawer tassel	snowdrop
Draw pulls	scarab, jasmin, violet, pansy, carnation, periwinkle, gentian
Key-rings	bee, butterfly, spring-beetle, tendril, umbel, sprigs, grape cluster, star, jet of water, corymbe
Key holes	dieclytra, hellebore, insect
Handles	barley, clematis, snail, winter cherry, bunch of grapes, corn, dahlia, narcissus
Feet	clematis, cirse

A biographical study of Gallé is beyond the scope of this book except to highlight the milestones in his furniture production. The cabinetmaking and marquetry atelier which he added to his glassworks at 39 Avenue de la Garenne in 1885 marked the beginning of a commercial operation which continued long after his death. In 1894 the workshop was 'industrialized', allowing Gallé to mechanize various stages of production, a decision which he felt necessary to defend in *La Revue des Arts Décoratifs* in 1900: 'new perspectives have been realized by the processes of carving, drilling, moulding and engraving by sandblasting, and gouging, all more rapid and economical than manually. The naturalist school should not ignore honest principles which offer inestimable advantages: extensions of a specialized and sober decor – that of furniture making – to all secondary parts where elaborate work can be replaced. The economics of the machine, as frequently seen in our epoch, provide a greater saving in costs than the additional grace and beauty warrants.' (Gallé had, of course, brought the same industrialization to his glassware, producing a wide range of etched vases and lamps for the commercial market.)

In 1906, in his obituary of Gallé in *La Revue Universelle: Littérature et Beaux-Arts*, Roger Marx drew attention to the two-tier quality of Gallé's furniture: 'Whereas a select number of pieces were designed for museums, others were vulgar, commercial and industrial, assembled with measured economy to reach every home.' The sad reality is that the revenue generated by Gallé's commercial furniture was indispensable to the cabinet shop's operation, in large part subsidizing the disproportionate time and artisanship spent on special pieces.

Daily production, especially between 1885 and 1890, allowed for small pieces such as tea-tables, screens, *sellettes*, nests of tables, and *guéridons*. Only in the 1890s did larger furniture begin to appear: *étagères*, vitrines, and entire *ensembles*. One tends to forget that Gallé began his furniture production long after his involvement in glass (*c.* 1874), and that it had not yet developed to the same stage of perfection. Later pieces, those shown from 1900, were infinitely more sophisticated than the earlier ones. His 1904 *Aube et Crépuscule* bed, for example, stands in the opinion of many as the epoch's *pièce de résistance*. Its symbolism and workmanship are unmatched. The bed was virtually the last piece of furniture that Gallé designed, apparently on the threshold of a new and immensely important phase in his furniture design.

Gallé was constantly reminded in the press that his furniture did not measure up to his glass. His responses were always immediate. An open letter to the critic Victor Champier in *La Revue des Arts Décoratifs* in 1900 was typical of the lengths to which he went to defend himself. The Paris critics, for the most part, however, nibbled away at what they considered a small, but fundamental, flaw. Maxime LeRoy expressed the general sense of misgiving in *L'Art*

Décoratif in his description of Gallé's umbel bedroom at the School of Nancy's 1903 Exposition in Paris. It was, he wrote, 'a sumptuous garden, infinitely elegant and perfumed . . . yet its construction lacks force. The flower is added to the architecture rather than being an integral part of it, as we would wish. Each time that I see Emile Gallé's furniture I am reminded inevitably of Anatole France. These two artists have the most extraordinary resemblance in terms of construction. For the author of Thaïs, the phrase is savoury: each epithet has inestimable value but the composition is never compact enough. One forgets the faults while reading; one lets oneself follow the charm of the story. Only when the book is closed does one think of criticizing . . . but then it is almost too late . . .'

One of the most severe criticisms has come with the perspective of time. Félix Marcilhac, in his 1981 booklet *Art Nouveau 1900*, wrote, 'more ceramicist and glassmaker than cabinetmaker, Emile Gallé did not succeed, in spite of all of his efforts, in creating a truly Art Nouveau piece of furniture. Only some works at the end of his life are exceptional . . . it is obvious that what concerned Gallé most in his furniture was not its structure, but rather its decorative value by using veneers of differently colored woods. He used them as a painter his easel, bringing together colors of every glittering and varied tone, to create totally realistic compositions. He basically only saw in his furniture a pretext for ornamental and symbolic research, being content to apply these to traditional shapes inherited from past centuries. . . .'

Unlike many of his contemporaries – especially Tiffany, who managed to keep the names of his designers a virtual secret for fifty years – Gallé was quick to promote his cabinetmakers and to give credit whenever due. The following, for example, were listed as collaborators in the 1903 School of Nancy catalogue: Louis Hestaux, Paul Holdenbach, Auguste Herbst, Paul Nicolas, Miss Rose Wild, Ismaël Soviot, and Emile Munier. On other occasions, especially in the early years, Gallé shared the credit with Prouvé.

Gallé exhibited his furniture frequently at the Salons, often showing entire rooms, to which vases and lamps were added in vitrines or on tables. In Nancy, he participated in the 1894 and 1904 Exposition de L'Art Décoratif Lorrain; in Paris, at the Société Nationale des Beaux-Arts from 1891 until his death, excluding 1896, 1899, and 1901; at both the 1889 and 1900 Exposition Universelle; and in the 1903 Exposition de l'Ecole de Nancy at the Pavillon de Marsan.

The following is a chronological (though inevitably incomplete) list of furniture which Gallé showed at these exhibitions and of pieces for which he had private commissions.

1889	Exposition Universelle (Paris)
	Poèmes Antiques, desk in robinia, in collaboration with V. Prouvé, inspired by Lecomte de Lille, purchased by M. Boucher of Cognac
	Jeux d'échecs, games table, in collaboration with V. Prouvé and L. Hestaux, purchased by M. P. Balaschoff
1890	Société Nationale des Beaux-Arts (Paris)
	Le Merisier de Sainte-Lucie, side-chair
1892	Société Nationale des Beaux-Arts (Paris)
	Commode *aux hortensias*, commissioned by Robert de Montesquiou
	Dining-room furniture, commissioned by M. Vasnier of Rheims
	Bedroom furniture *aux dahlias*
	Dining-room table, *herbes potagères*
1894	Société Nationale des Beaux-Arts (Paris)
	Fruits de l'esprit, cabinet
	Le Tabernacle du Saint Graal, cabinet, commissioned by Louis de Fourcauld
1895	Société Nationale des Beaux-Arts (Paris)
	Parfums d'autrefois, console
1900	Exposition Universelle (Paris)
	Les Granges, salon furniture comprising a settee, chair, and side-chair; based on the theme of cereals, corn poppies, potato flowers, *blé de mai*, and cranberries; purchased respectively by Mrs Waldeck-Rousseau, the Marquess of Bantés, and M. Lebeau
	Dining-room furniture, including the table *La Sève*
	La Blanche Vigne, buffet, clematis design
	Les Claudinettes, door curtain
	Les Ombellules, walnut *étagère*, purchased by M. Ridel for the Layal Museum
	Primevère, commode
	Pervenche, desk
	Orchidées Lorraines, desk
	Sagittaire, table
	Iris, table
	Bedroom furniture, *aux dahlias*
	Gaîne
	Commode *aux ipoméas*, purchased by the Kensington Museum
	La Forêt Lorraine, desk in *limodore des bois*, purchased by Mr Martin White of Dublin

1902   Société Nationale des Beaux-Arts (Paris)
        L'orge, commode
1903   School of Nancy Exposition at the Pavillon de Marsan (Paris)
        Exhibition vitrine, plant decoration
        La Vigne, vitrine
        La Lierre, vitrine
        La Montagne, cabinet
        Africa, bookcase in *bois des îles*
        Art Naturaliste, *étagère* (copy of *Les Ombellules*, exhibited at the
        1900 Exposition Universelle)
        Bedroom furniture, *aux ombellifères*
        Soleil et erable, door curtain
        Société Nationale des Beaux-Arts (Paris)
        Dining-room, including a *panetière*, buffet, dessert, and two chairs

1904   Exposition de l'Art Décoratif Lorrain (Nancy)
        Aube et Crépuscule, bed, commissioned by the magistrate M. Hirsch
        Vitrine *aux libellules*

Camille Gauthier

Born in Lorraine, Gauthier worked initially in Majorelle's cabinetmaking shop,
being listed in 1898 and 1899 at the Société des Arts français in Paris as
Majorelle's collaborator. An illustrated article in *La Lorraine Artiste* shows how
closely his furniture designs were influenced by those of Majorelle's when he
established his own studio on rue d'Auxonne in Nancy in 1901; so closely, in
fact, that Majorelle later resorted to litigation to prevent Gauthier from
reproducing his designs. Gauthier produced a wide range of small pieces of
furniture: mainly tea-tables, *guéridons*, screens and cabinets. These are invariably
light and gracious with pronounced Art Nouveau curves and pad feet. His
preferred woods were plane tree, walnut, beech, and Hungarian ash. Decoration was provided by veneered panels of cyclamens, Christmas roses, lilies-of-
the-valley, marguerites, and campanula within frames carved with matching
species. A 1901 vitrine set with a central *repoussé* leather panel of aquatic plants
by Edmond Lombard provided an interesting variation; later in the same year
Gauthier displayed a musician's library bookcase with lilac-coloured glass
panels at the exhibition of the Maison d'Art Lorraine. In 1903 the dining-room
table in tulipwood and walnut which he displayed at the School of Nancy's
exposition in Paris brought wide praise for its moulded legs with broad central
support. Also shown were a range of tiered tea-tables.

By 1905 Gauthier had taken on a partner, being listed as Gauthier, Poinsignon et Cie. The firm continued to exhibit at most of the Salons, even participating in the furniture competition for cheap furniture at the Grand-Palais in 1906. Reviews of their furniture appeared annually. In 1910 they displayed a lawyer's office in ash at the Salon d'Automne which included leather-upholstered chairs and carved eglantine decoration. A dining-room in fumed oak was carved with grape clusters. The earlier *fin-de-siècle* exuberance was gone; a quiet sobriety took its place.

Jacques Gruber

A professor at the Nancy School of Decorative Arts, Gruber maintained a nearby studio where he designed a wide range of objects, many of which were executed by fellow Nancy craftsmen, such as Férez, Schwartz, and Neiss. He is best known for his leaded stained-glass windows and etched glass panels, the latter a unique form of decoration which he frequently incorporated into his furniture. Gruber's furniture is similar to that of Vallin, with whom he collaborated on at least one occasion – the 1904 Exposition des Artistes de l'Est. His designs are, however, on a smaller scale and more varied; like Vallin's, his furniture is framed within deeply moulded and curved contours, but he also resorted to marquetry and, as mentioned, to glass panels etched with burgundy and pink landscapes.

In 1896, at the Salon de Nancy, Gruber displayed a tea-tray veneered with wheat stalks within a frame crisply carved with rose boughs. The next year a panel entitled *Le Soir* in enamelled and banded marquetry was illustrated in *La Lorraine Artiste*. In 1901 a three-leaf screen, purchased by the Hamburg Museum, showed his great versatility: an upper frieze of glass panels etched with clematis sprays emitted a soft translucency above panels of Japanese ash inlaid with cow parsley. A bed in Courbari wood illustrated in the same year was decorated with vines and poppies within a border of stylized sycamore seeds. The matching *armoire* offered a similar variety of flowers: clematis and cyclamen beneath a cornice of carved pine cones and roses. A desk displayed in 1903 drew criticism for its disharmony and lack of cohesion: Gruber had failed to compress the desk's various elements. It was, according to Gustave Soulier, 'more curious than logical'. The desk was part of an entire salon, including a three-panelled screen, mistletoe chandelier, and a ceramic chimney modelled in collaboration with Henri Gutton. A selection of leather-upholstered chairs, buffets, and *étagères* completed Gruber's display of furniture. Also shown were windows depicting convolvuli and clematis. The following year at the Exposition d'Art Décoratif Lorrain in Nancy, Gruber displayed a wide range of furniture, windows, vases, tableaux, and stoneware sculpture. His suite of *salon* chairs was upholstered in tooled leather. Absent, in large part, was the marquetry of his earlier furniture; influenced perhaps by Vallin, the emphasis was now more on richly varnished woods with sculpted details.

Henri Hamm

Hamm was one of the younger generation of Nanceian artisans to receive their apprenticeship under Gruber, Vallin, and Prouvé. A great deal of his work was, therefore, undertaken anonymously. Trained privately as a sculptor, Hamm worked also in other media. His furniture was strongly Art Nouveau in inspiration; curved structures were decorated with lightly carved floral sprays. The *armoire* which he exhibited in 1900 contained a cupboard door set with a textured glass panel intersected by four leaf-carved columns. In 1902 his display at the Société Nationale des Beaux-Arts included a reliquary which appeared a little too heavy. A year later, his dressing-table at the Salon d'Automne was charmingly conceived with a conical mirror above a serpentine top lightly carved with roses.

Today little of Hamm's work has been identified, a fine example, however, can be seen in the Ecole de Nancy.

Louis Hestaux

Hestaux was one of Gallé's earliest and most gifted cabinetmakers, collaborating in 1889 on a games table which Gallé exhibited at the Exposition Universelle. Initially an oil painter and watercolourist, Hestaux quickly became accomplished in other materials – copper, steel, glass, stone, leather, and wood – working primarily for Gallé and, from 1900, increasingly for himself. By 1904 their philosophies of art were sufficiently aligned for Hestaux to be heralded as the probable successor to the founder of the Nancy School, one whose work evoked the same blend of Japonisme, nature, and symbolism. He designed for other Nancy artists as well; for example, tapestries for Charles Fridrich and ceramics for the Mougin brothers.

Hestaux exhibited locally at the Société Lorraine des Amis des Arts and the Société de la Maison d'Art Lorraine, and in Paris at the Société Nationale des Beaux-Arts and the Société des Artistes français. He was awarded a silver medal for his furniture and a gold medal for his crystal at the 1900 Exposition Universelle. Three years later he participated in the School of Nancy's exposition at the Pavillon de Marsan.

In 1897 he showed a wooden bas-relief landscape panel and a mirror frame in which the sculpted details were heightened with brightly coloured enamels. A third panel depicted swirling plants in a characteristic Art Nouveau manner.

1 A marquetry panel on a Gallé vitrine at the Conservatoire National des Arts et Métiers, Paris, showing Gallé (far left) examining a vase being finished by one of his glass artisans. The panel is signed by Auguste Herbst, a cabinet-maker in Gallé's furniture studio.

2 Another marquetry panel from the vitrine in the Conservatoire National des Arts et Métiers. It shows Gallé (second from the right) instructing an artisan on glass decoration.

3 A detail of a Gallé marquetry desk top, showing the careful selection of burled and striated veneers to achieve a naturalistic effect.

4 A Gallé dragonfly table top showing various wood veneers. The dragonfly has inset mother-of-pearl eyes and abdomen.

5 One of two tablets in Gallé's *Les Chemins d'Automne* dessert on which cleaning instructions were listed. The words are incised into the wood in pokerwork fashion. (*Cf.* Ill. 68)

6 A Gallé marquetry table top with typical epithet. Notice the careful selection and range of veneers.

7 A humorous Gallé table top depicting a frog courtship scene (detail).

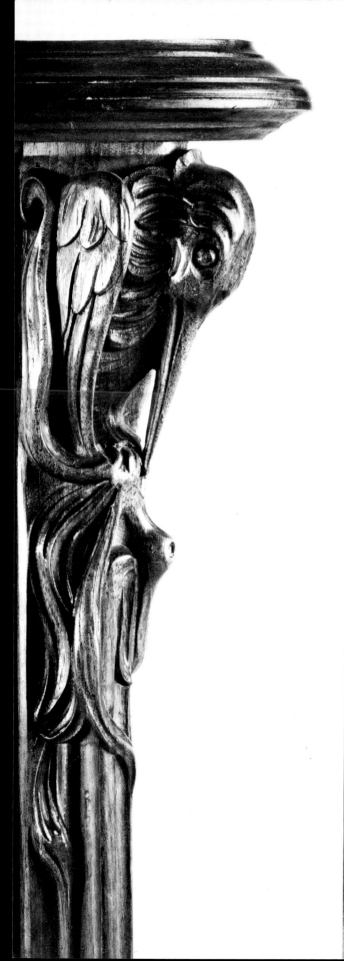

8 The capital of a Gallé vitrine, showing a crisply carved martin swallow (*pecheur-martin*).

9 A carved leg on Gallé's *herbes potagères* dining-room table, exhibited at the Société Nationale des Beaux-Arts in 1892. The table was illustrated in *La Revue Universelle de Littérature et Beaux-Arts*, 1905, p. 621.

10 The carved capital of a Majorelle tea table, depicting a spray of umbels.

11 The sculpted gallery on a Gallé desk. The central snail contains more carved detailing than the others.

12 The cornice of a Gallé vitrine, showing a frieze of dragonflies.

13 The frieze drawer on Gallé's *Les Fougères* vitrine. The carved insect has inset glass eyes. Illustrated in *Art et Industrie* in 1910, the vitrine is now in the Musée de l'Ecole de Nancy.

14 A bronze butterfly drawer pull on a Gallé end table.

15 One of the bronze key plates on Gallé's *Les Chemins d'Automne* dessert, providing Gallé with another means of imparting his message on "Nature".

16 A bronze door handle on a Horta cupboard showing the Belgian's whip-lash interpretation of Art Nouveau.

17 The bronze mount on the Guimard cupboard in the Musée des Arts Décoratifs, Paris. Incorporated in the long sinuous tendrils are a door handle and key plate.

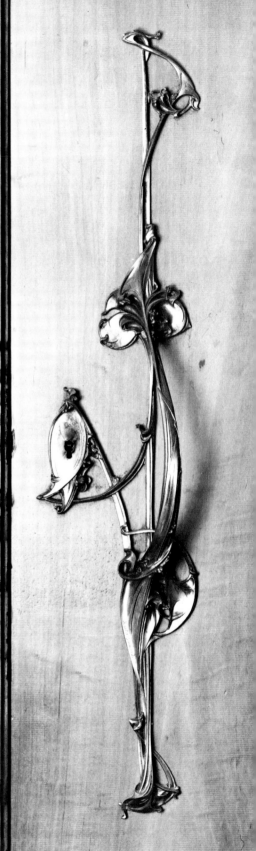

18 *Majorelle:* a cabinet with marquetry panel and wrought-iron mounts, shown at the 1903 Exposition of the Ecole de Nancy in Paris.

19 *Majorelle:* an undated photograph from Jules Majorelle's biography of his brother.

20 *Majorelle:* a dessert with marquetry back panel, pierced snail galleries, and ormolu goose drawer pulls.

21 *Majorelle*: a marquetry *cabinet de salon*.

22 *Majorelle*: a mahogany cabinet *aux orchidées*, with tambour doors and ormolu mounts. The back panel of the open shelf incorporates Majorelle's "fish-scale" marquetry design in locust wood.

23 *Majorelle: La Cascade*, a marquetry cabinet shown at the Société des Artistes français in 1899, in collaboration with Camille Gauthier. It was illustrated in *Art et Décoration*, July–December 1899, p. 4.

24 *Majorelle*: a *bureau-cartonnier* with applied flower-form glass lamps.

25 *Majorelle*: a superb desk incorporating twin lamps with glass shades, displayed at the Société des Artistes Français in 1903.

26 *Majorelle*: this mahogany desk with pine cone decoration (*Les Pins*) was shown at the Société des Artistes Décorateurs in 1904. It was illustrated in *Art et Décoration*, January–June 1904, p. 79, and in *L'Art Décoratif*, January–June 1905, p. 256.

27 *Majorelle*: this magnificent desk in amaranth and purplewood with twin lamps and ormolu orchid mounts was shown at the Salon in 1906.

28 *Majorelle*: mahogany desk and *chaise aux orchidées, c.* 1902.

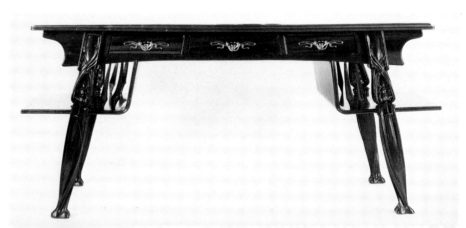

29 *Majorelle:* large *meuble d'appui* with wrought-iron mounts and grill over a glass-panelled door.

30 *Majorelle:* a longcase clock, *c.* 1905.

31 *Majorelle:* a carved and marquetry longcase clock.

32 *Majorelle:* this longcase clock, with ormolu orchid mounts and dial, was shown at the Société des Artistes Décorateurs.

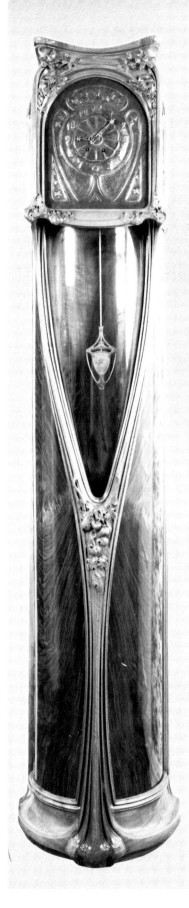

33 *Majorelle:* a mahogany cabinet *aux orchidées,* c. 1898.

34 *Majorelle:* a tea table with quarter-veneered top and pierced foliate legs and stretchers.

35 *Majorelle:* a tea table with pierced and carved floral frieze.

36 *Majorelle:* marquetry tea table.

37 *Majorelle:* two-tier mahogany tea table in the *fougère* pattern, illustrated in *Art et Décoration,* January–June 1903, p. 134, and in the firm's undated sales catalogue.

38 *Majorelle:* a mahogany and tamarind guéridon *aux nénuphars.* The model was shown at the 1903 Exposition of the Ecole de Nancy in Paris.

39 *Majorelle:* chest of drawers, part of the bedroom exhibited at the 1900 Exposition Universelle, illustrated in *Art et Décoration*, July–December 1900, p. 37, and in *L'Art Décoratif*, June 1900, p. 145.

40 *Majorelle:* one of a pair of *bergères* in *Les Pins* pattern, illustrated in the firm's undated sales catalogue.

41 *Majorelle:* a *canapé* in the *Les Pins* pattern.

42 *Majorelle:* a double bed *aux nénuphars*, illustrated in *Art et Industrie*, July 1909.

43 *Gallé:* a wall mirror *aux ombelles, c.* 1903.

44 *Gallé:* a contemporary photograph showing the salon *aux ombelles* commissioned by a Belgian client in 1903. The overmantel mirror and leather cushions incorporate the same umbel pattern. (*Cf.* also Pls *20* and *28*)

45 *Gallé:* two-tier marquetry tea table, *c.* 1903.

46 *Gallé:* the walnut étagère *Les Ombellules*, exhibited at the 1900 Exposition Universelle and the 1903 Exposition of the School of Nancy in Paris. The model was illustrated in *La Revue des Arts Décoratifs*, 1900, p. 289; *La Lorraine Artiste*, 1900, p. 113; and *Art et Décoration*, July–December 1900, p. 148.

47 *Gallé:* a side chair *aux ombelles.*

48 *Gallé:* a tabouret *aux ombelles, c.* 1903.

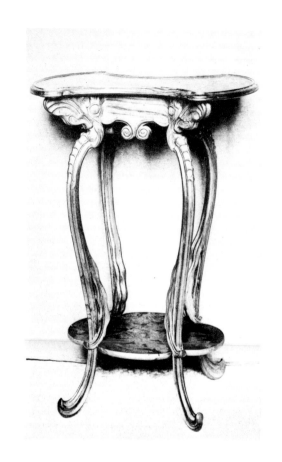

49 *Gallé:* a dragonfly chair, exhibited at the 1904 Exposition de l'Art Décoratif Lorrain in Nancy.

50 *Gallé:* a dragonfly guéridon, *c.* 1904.

51 *Gallé:* the famous 'Aube et Crépuscule' double bed commissioned by the magistrate Hirsch and displayed at the Exposition de l'Art Décoratif Lorrain in Nancy, 1904.

52 *Gallé:* marquetry table *aux libellules.* The model was discussed in *Le Figaro* in 1898.

53 *Gallé:* marquetry table *aux libellules.* This model is much rarer than the one with three legs.

54 *Gallé:* a marquetry jardinière now in the Musée de l'Ecole de Nancy. The design appears to be by Prouvé.

55 *Gallé: Les Parfums d'Autrefois*, a marquetry console exhibited at the Société Nationale des Beaux-Arts in 1895. It is now in the Musée de l'Ecole de Nancy.

56 *Gallé:* a marquetry *coffret* with bronze butterfly key plate.

57 *Gallé:* a marquetry *coffret* with bronze moth key plate.

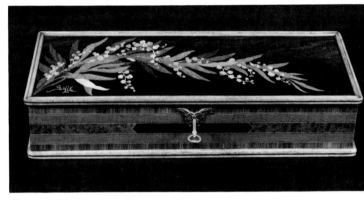

58 *Gallé: La Blanche Vigne*, the buffet with sculpted wild clematis and marquetry panels exhibited at the 1900 Exposition Universelle. The piece was illustrated in *La Lorraine Artiste*, 1900, p. 97, and *La Décoration et les Industries d' Art à l' Exposition de 1900*, 1900, p. 54.

59 *Gallé:* the small salon desk, *Les Ombelles*, exhibited at the 1900 Exposition Universelle.

60 *Gallé:* marquetry lady's desk *aux ombelles*.

61 *Gallé:* marquetry tea table *aux ombelles, c.* 1903.

62 *Gallé:* marquetry cabinet *aux grenouilles,* with frogs' leg feet and dragonfly upper gallery.

63 *Gallé:* marquetry umbrella stand *aux grenouilles.*

64 *Gallé:* marquetry cabinet with dragonfly cornice, *c.* 1900.

65 *Gallé:* marquetry screen with poppy finials. A similar model, now in the Musée de l'Ecole de Nancy, is illustrated in *Art et Décoration,* January–June 1898, p. 110.

66 *Gallé:* a wall étagère with carved and marquetry poppy decoration.

67 *Gallé:* marquetry table with poppy capitals and openwork frieze.

68 *Gallé: Les Chemins d'Automne*, an important buffet, *c.* 1893, in polychromed marquetry depicting "*La Vigne, L'été de la Saint-Martin, les Terres fortes, Souci des Champs, Septembre, Octobre*".

69 *Gallé*: a *canapé* and *chaise*, depicting various cereals, exhibited at the 1900 Exposition Universelle. Illustrated in *La Revue des Arts Décoratifs*, 1900, p. 42, and *La Lorraine Artiste*, 1900, p. 116.

70 *Gallé:* an *étagère* in the Chinese manner, now in the Musée de l'Ecole de Nancy.

71 *Gallé:* an early sculpted cabinet-on-stand, *c.* 1890, fitted with a cameo glass vase.

72 *Gallé:* a marquetry nest of tables with carved and pierced floral trestle ends.

73 *Gallé:* the table *sagittaire*, with arrowhead plant decoration, shown at the 1900 Exposition Universelle and illustrated in *La Revue des Arts Décoratifs*, 1900, p. 290, and 1901, p. 375. There is an example in the Musée de L'Ecole de Nancy.

74 *Gallé:* an early side chair, *Le Mérisier de Sainte-Lucie*, exhibited at the Société Nationale des Beaux-Arts in 1890.

75 *Gruber:* this screen, in etched glass with marquetry and sculpted wood panels, was exhibited at the 1903 Exposition of the Ecole de Nancy in Paris.

76 *Gruber:* the chimney exhibited at the 1903 Exposition of the Ecole de Nancy. Incorporating a ceramic panel by Bigot, it was modelled in collaboration with Henri Gutton.

77 *Gruber*: a detail of the headboard of a double bed, showing a characteristic three-panelled landscape in etched glass.

78 *Gruber*: desk and chair with leather upholstery and carved fern decoration, now in the Musée de l'Ecole de Nancy.

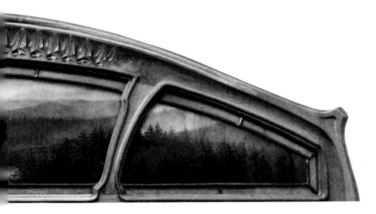

79 *Gruber*: Mirror carved with umbels and water lilies, now in the Musée de l'Ecole de Nancy.

80 *Gruber*: medal cabinet, now in the Musée de l'Ecole de Nancy.

81 *Gruber:* buffet with etched glass cornice, now in
the Musée de l'Ecole de Nancy.

His *pièce de résistance* was the *étagère* (see Ill. 82) he displayed at the 1901 Salon. In 1902 he showed four chairs with splats and seats upholstered in *repoussé* leather, each depicting local flora: dieclyta, caltha, gourds, and apple blossoms. There is a similar model in the Chrysler Museum of Art, Norfolk, Virginia.

Hestaux's furniture shows a lightness and grace often absent in the work of Nancy cabinetmakers. As the critic Emile Nicolas wrote in 1903, 'He personifies totally the intellectual product of Lorraine; his work reflects the aesthetics of our province with the utmost subtlety and discretion.' Unfortunately, very little has survived.

Georges Hoentschel

A ceramicist by profession, Hoentschel worked initially with Jean Carriès in his research on stoneware, exhibiting at the Salons of the Société Nationale des Beaux-Arts. After Carriès' death, Hoentschel moved to Montriveau where he worked with Emile Grittel. Contemporary reviews refer to him only as a potter, although he tried his hands at various other media.

An associate of Gallé, Hoentschel is best known for the *Salon des Eglantiers* which he exhibited at the 1900 Exposition Universelle. Taking the wild rose as his theme, he covered everything – mahogany chairs, tables and corner vitrines – with openwork thorny branches, evoking the praise of Lucien Magne who wrote that 'he enriches standard forms of construction . . . with a most gracious and free interpretation, doing away with corners and enhancing supports without reducing their function.' Other critics were less enthusiastic. Guillaume Janneau wrote later, of the same *boiserie*, that the spiky branches which enveloped the frame were so ubiquitous that one would more likely be preoccupied with where and how to sit than on sustaining lively conversation. Once again, an item's function had been subordinated to its appearance.

The furniture is now on display in the Musée des Arts Décoratifs in Paris beneath the large canvas *L'Ile Heureuse*, which Albert Besnard had been commissioned to paint for the Pavilion of the Central Union of Decorative Arts at the same Exposition.

Louis Majorelle

Majorelle was the indisputed master of Art Nouveau furniture, an opinion expressed by contemporary critics and even more assuredly today with the perspective that time affords. Blessed with superb design sense and technical virtuosity, he was simultaneously artist and artisan, designer and technician.

Majorelle's most fertile years were from 1898 to 1908, when piece after piece of breathtaking quality poured on to the market. Thereafter the standard dropped sharply, if not precipitously. The decision, taken between 1906 and

1908, to industrialize the workshops put an end to extravagance. Gone were the boldness and luxuriance of his ormolu waterlilies; in their place a wide range of lightly sculptured furniture for the public at large. Majorelle yielded to the post-1900 austerity of the middle-income market, a period of tightening budgets that ushered in the dreary furniture termed today euphemistically as 'transitional'.

One has to step beyond the Art Nouveau era to obtain any comparable sense of Majorelle's accomplishments. Few more exquisite pieces have been created at any time than his 1903 desk *aux orchidées* in amaranth and purpleheart with ormolu mounts and twin corolla glass lampshades (see Ill. 25). Equally spectacular and graceful was the longcase clock which he exhibited in 1901. Many other masterpieces likewise challenged the finest of Cressent, Riesener, Du Bois, and, later, Ruhlmann. The critics raved; nothing comparable had appeared in French furniture for a hundred years.

Despite the adulation, Majorelle was not immune from occasional censure. Gerdeil, in a long article in *L'Art Décoratif* in 1901, felt that the floral and landscape marquetry panels with which Majorelle decorated cupboard doors and beds were 'incompatible in subject-matter with the fundamental design of the piece and with its future home. Of all aspects of present Nancy art, these compositions are the most unfortunate.' Gerdeil went on to recommend that the empty spaces be left bare; the quality of the wood and the richness of its grain were beauty enough. Later, Majorelle's dining-room *aux tomates* and grand piano, exhibited at the 1904 Société Nationale des Beaux-Arts in Paris, were both found wanting by the critic Gustave Soulier. The design of the dining-room buffet (see Plate *1*) was too heavy and fundamentally incorrect: its abstract decorative line overpowered the piece's basic structure. In addition, the placement of the decorative wrought-iron hinges on the exterior doors made them practically invisible. With the piano (see Plate *8*), Majorelle and Prouvé had 'tried to make an object of beauty out of . . . a grand piano! Where Charpentier and Besnard have failed, so have they.'

The critics found comparison between Majorelle and Gallé inevitable. Whereas Majorelle lacked the passion for nature and the intellectualism of his neighbour, he was clearly more accomplished as a cabinetmaker. He also, most importantly, adhered to the traditional rules of furniture design handed down through the centuries. The great criticism levelled at Gallé was that he transformed the superstructures and legs of his furniture into tree trunks and branches and, even, monstrous dragonflies. Majorelle judiciously stayed within established limits, applying his floral decoration to conventional supports. Gallé went about it backwards, transforming trees into pieces of furniture *before* considering the pieces' function.

Analysis of contemporary art reviews suggests that Majorelle placed less emphasis on the annual Paris Salons than his fellow Nanceians. Though he was a long-standing member of four – the Société des Artistes français, the Société Nationale des Beaux-Arts, the Société des Artistes Décorateurs, and the Salon d'Automne – he appears to have concentrated more on selling his furnishings directly to the public than on exhibiting them beforehand. In 1898 his letter heading listed four retail outlets – Nancy, Paris, Vosges and Cannes-Alpes Maritimes. By 1910 the two last-mentioned had been replaced by larger cities, Lille and Lyon. The firm also published a valuable undated catalogue (*c.* 1910) in which a wide range of lamps, vases and furniture were illustrated. Ensembles were grouped by category and theme. For example, bedrooms were offered in clematis, lilac, fern, seaweed, and rose patterns; boudoirs in hawthorn and pine cone. Single pieces, such as tea-tables and plant stands, were carved with honesty, strawberry creepers, convolvuli, bell flowers, mistletoe, woodbine, silphium and arrowheads.

As a cabinetmaker, Majorelle's knowledge of woods and veneers was prolific. Unlike Gallé, whose preference was for soft, pale woods inlaid with stained fruitwoods, Majorelle chose dark hardwoods. The range seems endless, each carefully selected for the piece's function – bedrooms, for example, are comfortable and intimate, requiring a wood with a warm, reddish hue. Favourites included walnut, mahogany, palissander, amaranth, purpleheart, thuya, and teak. Veneers were exotic, many cultivated to Majorelle's specifications in Marrakesh: banana, coconut palm, *bois des îles*, locust-wood, and bougainvillea. To these could be added mother-of-pearl, brass and metal inlays for major commissions, such as the bedroom which Majorelle exhibited at the 1900 Exposition Universelle.

Furniture mounts were either in gilt-bronze (ormolu) or wrought-iron. Majorelle placed great pride in his bronzeware. Two full pages in the School of Nancy's 1903 Exposition catalogue were reserved for illustrations of his floral drawer pulls and key plates. It was his ormolu waterlily and orchid mounts, however, that put the stamp of genius on this aspect of Majorelle's cabinetwork. Introduced in 1898, they were applied *en série* to salon and library ensembles as capitals, *chutes* and *sabots*. The effect was immensely lavish. Surprisingly, in view of their universal popularity today, they were found by the critic Gerdeil in 1901 to be excessive, 'reminding one of the gaudiness of France's eighteenth-century cabinetmakers'.

Majorelle's choice of wrought-iron for furniture mounts came from his satisfaction in its use for electric lamp standards. Several series of furniture – for example, *La Mer*, *La Vigne*, *Sagittaires* and *Tomates* – incorporated grey-patinated iron mounts in preference to bronze. The floor lamp with thuya motif that was commissioned by the students of the Lycée at Bar-le-duc for the President of the Republic shows the mastery that Majorelle achieved in this medium; likewise his balcony for the Galerie Lafayette in Paris.

The workshops at La Maison Majorelle produced nearly everything that was required: not only furniture and metalware, but marbles, plaster, leather, fabrics and lace. Ancillary materials were commissioned from local artisans: the Daums produced the glass shades for his lamps, while Bigot met his ceramic needs till 1905, after which these were provided by the Mougin brothers and Cytère in nearby Rambervillers.

The following chart lists Majorelle's life and career chronologically. Pieced together from numerous sources – most particularly the biography by his brother Jules – it is intended to highlight the important events in Majorelle's furniture career.

1859 Born on 27 September, in Toul, the eldest of eight children.

1860 Auguste Majorelle, his father, moved to Nancy where he established a modest decorating business in the rue Callot in the Faubourg Saint-Pierre. Mainly ceramics and furniture were produced.

1875 Louis Majorelle exhibited a painting at his first Salon.

1877 Entered the School of Beaux-Arts in Paris, studying under Jean-François Millet.

1878 Father moved his business to larger premises on the rue Girardet.

1879 Father died, forcing Louis to cancel his studies and return to Nancy to take over the family business.

1879–89 In partnership with his brother Jules, continued to produce the range of Louis XV- and XVI-style pieces which their father had manufactured. The business premises were again moved, this time to 6 rue de Vieil-Aître.

1889 Exhibited a large sleigh-form bed at the Exposition Universelle.

c. **1894** First attempts to produce furniture in the 'new' style. A table, entitled *La Source*, contained a floral marquetry top inscribed with a verse by Théophile Gautier:

> '*Peut-être deviendrai-je un fleuve*
> *Baignant vallon, rochers et tours*'.

1897 Enlarged cabinetmaking and wrought-iron ateliers constructed by Lucien Weissenburger behind Majorelle's villa on the rue du Vieil-Aître.

1898–99 Introduction of elaborate *nénuphar* and *orchidée* ormolu furniture mounts.

1899 Displayed two cabinets, *La Cascade* and *Les Baigneuses*, at the Société des Artistes français.

1900	Exhibit at the Exposition Universelle included a bedroom, dining-room, and selection of library furniture.
1901	Displayed a longcase clock and *armoire*-bookcase at the Société des Artistes français.
1902	Participation in the Salon des Industries du Mobilier at the Grand-Palais, Paris.
1903	Participation in the School of Nancy's exposition at the Pavillon de Marsan, Paris.
1904	Exhibit at the Société Nationale des Beaux-Arts included a dining-room *aux tomates* and a grand piano in collaboration with Victor Prouvé.
1904–05	Exhibited at the Exposition d'Art Décoratif Lorrain in Nancy.
1906	Exhibit at the Société des Artistes Décorateurs included a library in *Les Pins* pattern and a salon *orchidées*.
1906–08	Industrialization and modernization of the ateliers to provide for larger volume of low-priced furniture.
1910	Bedroom exhibited at the Salon d'Automne.
1911	Bedroom and dining-room exhibited at the Salon d'Automne.
1916	The bombing of his atelier during the war forced Majorelle to leave Nancy. He exstablished himself in the Studio Julian, Paris, where he continued to do interior design work.
1918	Returned to Nancy to rebuild his ateliers. Post-war styles had changed, however, and his production lacked both its earlier originality and quality.
1925	As a member of the Jury, Majorelle exhibited a library *hors concours* at the Exposition Universelle.
1926	Died on 15 January. Alfred Lévy, a student of his, took over the artistic direction of La Maison Majorelle.

Victor Prouvé

Nancy's most versatile artist – a true Renaissance man in the view of contemporary critics – Prouvé was also most willing to share his abundant knowledge with the region's next generation, a quality which made him the automatic choice to succeed to the head of the School of Nancy on Gallé's death. Prouvé's talents touched on all the arts – graphics and sculpture on his own and numerous other media in partnership; for example, leather bookcovers with Camille Martin and René Wiener; jewelry with Charles Rivaud; fabrics with Courteix; wrought-iron with Emile Robert; ceramics with the Mougin brothers; embroidery with Fridrich; and furniture with Vallin and Gruber.

Born on 13 August 1858 in Nancy, Prouvé entered the School of Beaux-Arts in 1871. On graduating in 1877, he joined the studio of the painter Cabanel in Paris. For ten years, Prouvé concentrated on painting, while remaining closely in touch with the decorative arts through his father, who was employed as a modeller for Emile Gallé's father, M. Gallé-Reinemer. The two sons became fast friends and collaborators, and it was clearly Gallé's enthusiasm that persuaded Prouvé to experiment with other art forms. Two early furniture works were an oak cabinet with bas-relief panels based on Lecomte de Lisle's *The Lorraine Oak, a French work*, and a marquetry table, part of a series on ancient history entitled *The Rhine Separates the Gauls from all of Germany*, both of which were exhibited at the 1889 Exposition Universelle and later at the Salon du Centenaire des Beaux-Arts. From that point on, Prouvé plunged into all facets of the decorative arts, collaborating with virtually every Nancy craftsman on projects for forthcoming exhibitions. In furniture, he worked most closely with Vallin, sculpting the friezes and panels on *armoires* and beds. His work with Gruber was similar, though less pronounced.

At the 1903 Nancy Exposition in Paris, Prouvé showed two panels in *repoussé* leather, one entitled *Fructidor*, another (see Ill. 83) now in the Musée de l'Ecole de Nancy, and his famous bronze coupe *La Nuit* belonging to a M. Meyer-Guillau. He also collaborated with Rivaud on a selection of metal jewelry.

Eugène Vallin

Vallin was born in 1856 in Herbéviller, a suburb of Blamant. His family moved to Nancy where he was indentured in an uncle's cabinetmaking factory which specialized in ecclesiastical furnishings. It was at this time that Vallin read Viollet-le-Duc's *Dictionnaire d'Architecture*, a treatise on which he built his own philosophies of design. On the completion of his apprenticeship, he took a modelling course at Nancy's School of Design, concentrating on Gothic church architecture.

Early commissions included an enamelled altar and a pair of bronze church doors. In 1883 Vallin sculpted the confessional for a chapel in Bonsecours. Four years later, he designed and executed a large organ for the Church of St Léon in Nancy. Other commissions followed quickly: the Church of Notre Dame of St Dié, the Cathedral of St Ségolène in Metz, and, in collaboration with P. Charbonnier, the Maison de Peuple in Nancy. All of Vallin's work until this time was heavily Gothic in inspiration; a sideboard exhibited at the 1894 Nancy Exposition of Art incorporated the architectural spires and dentilled cornice of a fourteenth-century piece of furniture. Vallin's conversion to Art Nouveau design must, therefore, have occurred almost overnight, as the house and studio which he built and furnished for himself in 1896 varied only marginally from his designs fifteen years later. The front door, carved with a central spray of umbels surrounding a letter box by his friend and collaborator, Victor Prouvé, is now in the Ecole de Nancy. Unsigned, it is indistinguishable from the work of many of his Nancy contemporaries. Façades completed at the same time for the houses of the architect Biet on the rue de la Commanderie and Dr Aimé on rue St Dizier have survived to bear witness to Vallin's radical stylistic change. Where previously there were Gothic architraves and buttresses, now philodendrons and hortensia adorn the outlines of Vallin's buildings.

Unlike most other Nancy cabinetmakers, he does not appear ever to have used marquetry to provide his decorative effect, preferring carved figural panels. Vallin's versatility was soon evident. He designed shop-windows for the haberdasher Delchard and the merchant Vaxelaire, the latter in collaboration with Charles André. By 1900, he had even managed to fit in a special request from Emile Gallé to make a doorway portal for the Gallé Studio on which would be carved the master's defiant proclamation to the artistic world, '*ma racine est au fond des bois*'.

It is for his furniture that Vallin is now known. His pieces are recognizable by their monumentality and deeply moulded and fluid contours. He relied on top-quality woods and the interplay of light along their curved surfaces for decorative effect, only occasionally incorporating carved figural or floral panels. Several of his masterpieces – for example, the dining-room for M. Masson, which included a massive fireplace surmounted by Prouvé's frieze of a naked maiden amongst branches, and his celebrated multi-purpose, multi-media bench/bookcase/cupboard described in 1902 by Emile Nicolas in *La Lorraine* as a 'cabinet de travail' – are now in the Musée de l'Ecole de Nancy. Another important piece in the Museum's collection is Vallin's minister's desk which drew wide acclaim when it was first exhibited in 1902. Vallin participated in the School of Nancy's 1903 Exposition in Paris and the Exposition of the Société Lorraine des Amis des Arts the following year.

In 1904 he designed, with the architect Munier, the building in which the Exposition of Decorative Arts in Nancy was held, also displaying several suites of furniture. Later works of note included a billiard salon in 1910 for a client in Rupt-sur-Moselle, Vosges, and, in the same year, at the Salon d'Automne, a reception room which was purchased by Art et Industrie for its Paris office. Vallin retained the same vigorous lines and grand sweep in these later works. He died in 1922.

30

31

32

34

35

36

37

38

Paris

Paris, unlike Nancy, did not have its own school or principal group. The city was simply too large and diverse for a single theme in the decorative arts to dominate. Most Art Nouveau exponents, however, operated within loosely defined limits of style; the Salons kept them in touch with prevailing fashions. Only Carabin and Guimard kicked over convention's traces entirely.

One is surprised, when reading contemporary art reviews, at the large number of cabinetmakers in Paris who either regularly, or intermittently, designed Art Nouveau furniture. The number is close to fifty, indicating to what extent the style pervaded the capital between 1895 and 1905. The most important of these are discussed in this book, the criteria for inclusion being the individual's participation in, and exposure at, the Salons, and the importance placed on his work by the critics, then and now. Among those whose works are omitted are the following: Jansen, Binet, Magne, Dumas, Guérin, Bonvallet, Bec, Ducrot, Péjac, Richard, Dubuisson, Jaulmes, Verneuil, Rigaud, Pomeroy, Charbonnier, François, and Turcq. All of these, and more, made Art Nouveau furniture of lesser importance. Also omitted are the works of three most gifted designers, Paul Follot, Maurice Dufrêne, and Léon Jallot, whose careers began after 1900 with a selection of lightly inspired Art Nouveau furnishings, but who grew to maturity and importance in the Art Déco era.

The annual Salons provided an irreplaceable opportunity for cabinetmakers to display their latest works. The Salons became, in fact, *de rigueur*: the critics seldom strayed beyond the Champs-de-Mars or the Grand-Palais, and their opinions, published mostly in *Art et Décoration* and *L'Art Décoratif*, could spell success or oblivion. Other important stepping-stones in the careers of Art Nouveau furniture designers were Samuel Bing's Maison Art Nouveau and his pavilion at the 1900 Exposition Universelle; Julius Maier-Graefe's La Maison Moderne; the exhibitions of *L'Art dans Tout* (formerly *Les Cinq* and then *Les Six*); and, of course, the 1900 Exposition Universelle.

Paris Art Nouveau furniture was distinctly different in style from that of rival Nancy. In the capital, nature was frequently stylized: the sweep of Landry's cornices or Plumet's supports echoed a plant's vitality and synthesis. Only a hint of its inspiration was necessary, whereas in Nancy the flower was slavishly reproduced, often down to its pistils and stamens.

Designers in the two centres often derided each other for their respective attitudes. Guimard, for example, renounced flowers and animals as a decorative theme in an 1898 article in *Le Figaro*. Gallé, clearly wounded, responded immediately 'against discounters of *snobisme* who wish to introduce the French, after the Belgians and the Germans, to cosmopolitan modernism ... [which is] a false art if one can describe as art such a deformation of nature's themes at the hands of a cabinetmaker's chisel.'

Eugène Gaillard, in his treatise *A Propos du Mobilier*, likewise found a moment to denigrate the Nanceians, 'earthworms, macaroni, iris, mistletoe, holly, thistle, and seaweed, which lately has enveloped everything . . . the nude covered by a thousand diverse insects, the dragonfly in one moment swarming and in another flying above it all . . . the slimness – O what slimness! – of the androgynous maidens, their noses emerging from maelstroms of hair, their dilated yellow eyes above broad mouths . . . these are for the public the landmarks of our modern revolution.' Such spats aside, Paris and Nancy presented a united front to the rest of the world, settling down after 1900 to an uneasy coexistence and sharing pavilions at the Turin and Munich Expositions.

Unfortunately, a great deal of the furniture produced in Paris was unsigned, leaving one with the difficult task of identification. Landry, Sauvage, Gallerey, and the Selmersheims, for example, produced furniture through the years which is today indistinguishable. To this problem must be added the industrial furniture manufacturers and retailers of the Faubourg Saint-Antoine who plagiarized the works of the foremost designers.

Albert Angst

Angst left the School of Nancy in the mid-1890s to study under Jean Dampt in Paris. The move appears to have been propitious; the oak secretary which he exhibited in 1897 showed great originality and charm. Entitled 'Song of the Evening and Morning', it was elaborately carved with larks, roosters and nocturnal birds saluting the dawn above a frog-infested pond. Two years later, as a member of the Society *L'Art dans Tout* at the Galerie de la rue Caumartin, he displayed a chair which, although too heavy and of slightly illogical conception, was taken as clear indication by the critics that Angst had benefited enormously from his stay in Dampt's studio.

He continued to participate in the annual *L'Art dans Tout* Salons, exhibiting alongside Sauvage, Sorel, and Charpentier. In 1902 his *médaillier* cabinet at the Salon Nationale des Beaux-Arts incorporated a gently flaring Art Nouveau frame which enclosed four wood panels above root-carved feet. The following year Angst's lady's desk showed a cleaner look; the tendency of his earlier Nancy training to over-ornamentation had been largely eliminated. A seven-piece dining-room suite in walnut was panelled in ash and elm. The buffet contained two upper cupboard doors crisply carved in high relief with panels representing 'The Family' and 'Work' in a distinctly Vallin style.

Very little of Angst's furniture has been identified, largely because he evidently did not sign his work.

Henri-Jules-Ferdinand Bellery-Desfontaines (1867–1910)

A student of Jean-Paul Laurens, Bellery-Desfontaines was an accomplished painter whose canvases were exhibited annually in the 1890s at the Champs-Elysée. From 1897 he began also to concentrate on furniture design, bringing to each project a rare conscientiousness. In planning a piece, he had a scaled wax maquette fashioned from which the wooden prototype was made.

Bellery-Desfontaines mixed a strange blend of medievalism and provincialism with modernism: massive rudimentary structures were enhanced with Art Nouveau motifs, often introduced as large hinges and brackets cast as sprays of columbine or ivy. The walnut table which he displayed in 1897 incorporated an elaborate interlocking network of stretchers and brackets carved with water-cress which supported a tiled ceramic top. The predominant effect was one of strength with quiet elegance. Another model, executed by the cabinetmaker Lemale and shown the following year at the Société des Artistes français, was more robust; the tripod frame was lightly accentuated with carved vine leaves beneath a ceramic top by Clement Massier decorated with purple and crimson grape clusters. Bellery-Desfontaines sought the advice of Henri Rapin in these early experimental works.

Bellery-Desfontaines' entry at the 1900 Exposition Universelle included a table, clock, and casket which were marketed by the Maison Bellangé. His bedroom suite at the 1907 Salon of the Société Nationale des Beaux-Arts left the critics both confused and appalled by its overtaxed ornamentation. The bed's headboard was designed as a large apple tree laden with gold fruit; the *armoire* included copper key escutcheons and *repoussé* panels which competed visually with wrought-iron hinges and brackets executed by Szabo-Renou. A psyche, fauteuil, and desk completed the ensemble, which had to be viewed in its entirety for each individual piece not to appear overly rich and ornate. Like that of Guimard, Bellery-Desfontaines' furniture should not be judged outside of its original setting.

Possibly stung by the censure aroused by such work, Bellery-Desfontaines turned to pieces which were largely stripped of their ornamentation. The dessert which he showed in 1910 has a stark rationality; it is still perhaps too large but lacks the previous richness. He died in the same year.

Eugène Belville

The Lorraine cabinetmaker, Eugène Belville, moved to Paris where he became a versatile participant at the annual Société Nationale des Beaux-Arts Salons at the turn of the century. His preferred medium was tooled and *repoussé* leather with which he enhanced his furniture, such as the mahogany cartonnier shown in 1902.

Belville's masterpiece was the chimney surround with flanking seats which he displayed at the 1898 salon. Its influence was strongly medieval; the chimney was crowned with an elaborate pediment that resembled the pointed arch of a tabernacle. Twin high-backed choirstall seats extended on each side, stiffly traditional in form yet sumptuously decorated with carved floral cartouches. Curiously, the critics were in accord on its innovative qualities, although Guillaume Janneau had it in mind when he wrote that designers tend to lose sight of an object's intended function in trying to pioneer a new style. The chimney was later exhibited at the 1900 Exposition Universelle.

Belville's 1902 mahogany piano – again with *repoussé* leather panels – was less successful. A broad line parallel to, and above, the keyboard, was repeated at the foot, producing a grossly overworked effect. In 1904 an *armoire* in Hungarian ash proved more successful.

Léon Benouville

Benouville was an architectural engineer who formed his own company, Arts et Manufactures Benouville, in the 1890s to produce furnishings for the houses which he designed. His early Art Nouveau furniture had a distinctly personal touch. Spidery legs support table tops and writing surfaces veneered in pearwood with flower sprays flanked by brass mounts cast amusingly as slender praying mantises and beetles. Lightness and charm pervade all of Benouville's work. By 1900, however, he had identified himself with modestly priced furniture for the modestly paid working-man. His furniture became more rational, eliminating to a large extent the superfluous decoration which had made it so delightful. The 1900 Exposition Universelle proved an important forum. Positioned alongside Plumet and Tony Selmersheim, Landry, and Sorel, Benouville exhibited two complete suites of furniture, both in unseasoned mahogany decorated with large chased or *repoussé* copper panels in what the critic Charles Saunier described as 'most remarkable . . . and in the best taste.' Further praise came from G.-M. Jacques who wrote, 'His works are, above all, works of reason where everything is subordinated to his respect for physical laws. In M. Benouville we have the engineer sensing that the time has come when the man of science must make an artist of himself.'

By 1901, Benouville's enthusiasm for Art Nouveau decoration had grown cooler. His bedroom at the Société Nationale des Beaux-Arts included modest floral marquetry and scrolled feet. Everything looked most affordable. The furniture was displayed in bare rooms, leading to an exchange of letters in *L'Art Décoratif* in which Benouville replied to the editor's charge of bleakness by explaining, by means of an exhaustive chart which listed the room sizes of an average Parisian house, that ancillary decoration detracted from the elegance of the furnishings. Benouville's entries at the 1902 Salon included a coffee table and revolving bookcase, both rational, elegant and with minimum ornamentation. Benouville was by then a member of La Société d'Art par et pour le Peuple. He died in 1908.

Louis Bigaux

Louis Bigaux, an interior decorator, and Joseph Le Coeur, a furniture designer, formed a partnership in the 1890s to produce a range of interiors at prices affordable to the bourgeoisie. William Morris's diatribes against the evils of the machine had proved inapplicable to furniture manufacture. Whereas it could not match the quality of hand-made furniture (nor did it try), machine manufacture could bring a slightly inferior product to a much wider, and less discerning, public.

In 1897 Bigaux and Le Coeur showed three complete interiors at the annual Salon of *La Libre Esthétique* in Brussels. The critics were suitably tolerant, passing over the modest designs and lightly carved decoration of the furnishings to emphasize what the economics of machine production *could* achieve, rather than what it could *not*. The philosophy of modern art was allied to that of simplicity. Le Coeur's furniture, in bleached oak inlaid with *bois des îles* parquetry, was in harmony with the subtle colourations of Bigaux's lavender and yellow upholstery, wall-papers, and fireplace surround. In 1898 the pair completed a similar suite of rooms for the restaurant Voisin in Paris. The dominant theme – green chestnut branches with gold fruit – was carried through to the brass key plates on the doors. By 1900, Bigaux had emerged as the head of the firm, receiving generous coverage and praise from the critics for his display at the Exposition Universelle. Established as a pioneer of industrial furniture design, his exhibition was closely analysed in *Art et Décoration* by Gustave Soulier, who made only brief mention at the end of his article of the neighbouring exhibit of a Mr Samuel Bing who was pursuing the same goals of revolutionary technology and design! Bigaux harnessed the talents of numerous young artists and artisans to create his interiors: listed as painters were Rudnicki, Seguin, Bordère, and Brunet; as sculptors, Eugène Baguès, Firmin Bate, and Hermant; Isidore Leroy (wallpapers), Alexandre Bigot (ceramics), Poincet (marbles), while Le Coeur continued to oversee furniture design.

In 1902 Bigaux's exhibit at the Société Nationale des Beaux-Arts brought censure for its incorporation of painted furniture, believed by some to be a violation of the wood's natural beauty. In addition, the designs of his Art Nouveau chairs and *canapés* were considered excessive; the critic Roger de Félice bemoaned the fact that the serpentine armrests and seat-rails did nothing to add to their comfort. He wrote, 'Once again one sees talented artisans wasting their talents . . .' Further criticism awaited Bigaux at the 1906 Salon of the Société des Artistes Décorateurs. His young girl's bedroom in white-painted ash, sycamore, and plane-tree was considered a misuse of the medium rather than avant-garde. Five years later, at the 1911 Salon d'Automne, Bigaux's perseverance was rewarded. His painted furniture was seen as quietly refined and charming, a clear precursor of the post-World War I fashion for brightly japanned or lacquered interior decoration.

Joseph Boverie

Boverie was an accomplished cabinetmaker who exhibited only briefly at the Parisian Salons. His walnut buffet and chimney, shown in 1901 at the Société des Arts Réunis at the Georges Petit gallery, brought praise from the critic Gustave Soulier for the novel manner in which Boverie applied pendant gilt-bronze blossoms to the sculpted branches which grew in profusion over every surface. The pieces lack spontaneity, however; their over-ornateness creates a heaviness which overpowers their fine craftsmanship. His lady's desk (see Ill. 146) is more successful.

Rupert Carabin

Carabin's work can be divided broadly into three phases: seemingly endless controversy and confrontation during his lifetime; nearly total oblivion – if not purgatory – from the time of his death in 1932 until the sale in 1969 at the Hôtel Drouot of the furniture commissioned in 1890 by his first client, M. Henry Montandon; and, since then, a fervent treasure hunt by today's collectors to uncover his lost works.

Carabin was born in Saverne, Alsace, on 17 March 1862. Ten years later, the family moved to Paris where Carabin trained as a stone engraver while studying design in the evenings. In 1878, he became a wood sculptor at a furniture-maker's in the Faubourg St Antoine. His career was punctuated along the way with controversy. In 1882 his sculpture 'A Republic', depicting mouldings from a mortician's business, was refused by the Salon; in 1890 his bookcase for Montandon was again barred, this time by the jury of the Salon des Indépendants, the very group which had broken away from the Salon des Artistes français to eliminate the limits on artistic expression which it now applied to Carabin, one of its founder members! Clearly, colleagues such as Puvis de Chavannes, Rodin, Besnard, and Cazin were not amused at what they considered an aesthetic transgression.

Along the way, Carabin was commissioned to create a wide range of furniture, almost exclusively for private clients such as Albert Kahn, the founder of the Bois de Boulogne, and, in 1900, an upright piano for the comedian Coquelin-Cadet of the Comédie-française. These, following his banishment from the Salon des Indépendants, were displayed at the Société Nationale des Beaux-Arts.

Carabin's studio was at 22 rue Turbigo. Here he participated, with a small team of fellow artisans, in every stage of his commissions for bronzes, ceramics, and furniture. The last-mentioned were carved from pearwood, oak and, especially, walnut. The finished item was first impregnated with linseed oil and then polished at great length with powder to bring out the wood's rich grain. Carabin's dominant furniture theme was the nude female form. This he incorporated into virtually every piece, either as kneeling caryatids supporting tables and chairs or in carved panels on cupboard doors. His interpretation was slightly vulgar in its realism: the figures are heavy, with serious faces and hair swept up into chignons.

Nobody questioned Carabin's technical skills. As a sculptor, his work was of the first rank. It was the use of furniture as a medium for his sculpture that aroused such censure. The critic Gerdeil summarized the resentment when he wrote, in reviewing Carabin's furniture at the 1901 Salon of the Société Nationale des Artistes, that 'one must protest the illegitimacy of transforming something into something else. Why, in wishing to create figural sculpture, does he put it on the foot of a table or the side of a piano? A piano has no relationship to a nude woman and she, in turn, makes a mockery of it. The maidens of Vallgren, Charpentier, and Rivière look very good on their own; those of Carabin have equally pleasant dispositions. Why therefore must they infringe on areas of the decorative arts where they do not belong?'

This argument recurred many times, voiced by the critics Max Nordeau, Roger Marx, Paul Gsell, Gustave Geffroy, and Arsène Alexandre in tones ranging from curious to indignant. All felt that decoration must relate to the object which it enhances. The female form was by tradition suited to jewelry and vases, not to furniture and lamps. The artist who failed to comprehend this relationship violated his medium.

In 1896, Louis de Fourcauld expanded on this in the *Revue des Arts Décoratifs* when he suggested that 'M. Carabin's allegorical table and chair would no doubt be of interest in a museum, but can one imagine them as part of one's daily life?' Carabin's furniture appeared to be suitable for exhibition purposes *only*; it could not be integrated into a living environment.

Today, thanks largely to the 1969 Montandon sale, as mentioned, and the retrospective exhibition at the Galerie du Luxembourg in 1974, Carabin is finally in vogue. No major Art Nouveau furniture collection can be considered complete without an example of his work.

39 *Colonna*: the marquetry music cabinet displayed in Bing's Pavilion at the 1900 Exposition Universelle. Illustrated in *Art et Décoration*, July–December 1900, p. 44; *The Studio*, XX, 1900, p. 166; and *La Revue des Arts Décoratifs*, 1900, p. 261.

40 *Charpentier and Selmersheim*: mantel clock displayed at the Salon of the Libre Esthétique in Brussels, 1899. Illustrated in *Art et Décoration*, January–June 1901, p. 101.

41 *Charpentier*: parcel-gilt bronze mantel clock.

42 *Gaillard*: dressing table and chair, *c.* 1903.

43 *Landry*: desk, *c.* 1904.

44 *Guimard*: boudoir chair in pearwood.

45 *Guimard*: pearwood buffet, *c.* 1906.

46 *Serrurier-Bovy*: buffet, *c.* 1900.

47 *Horta*: dining-room now in the Musée Horta on the rue Americain, Brussels. The silver candlesticks are by Fernand Dubois.

48 *Homar*: mahogany double bed and night-table with carved and pierced rosebud crest and angles, the panels veneered in various fruitwoods, the women's features sculpted in low relief.

49 *Clapés*: giltwood vitrine, now in the Museo Gaudí at the Park Güell, Barcelona.

43

44

45

46

48

49

Alexandre Charpentier

Few Art Nouveau exponents embraced the concept of the Belle Epoque maiden more fervently than Charpentier. Invariably plump, if not distinctly overweight, these nymphs frolic or recline on nearly all of Charpentier's work, whether belt-buckles, pewter vases, *armoires*, or key escutcheons.

A founder-member of *Les Cinq*, Charpentier was trained in his home town of Liège as a sculptor. Association with Dampt and Plumet, however, quickly led him into related fields. Early essays included a porcelain wine jug and creamer in 1897 and, a year later, the bathroom mural in enamelled faience on which he and Félix Aubert collaborated. Produced at the Sarreguemines pottery works, it is now in the Musée de l'Ecole de Nancy. Other items included a silver portrait medallion of Ernest Besnard and an embossed leather flask. In 1899, the clock which he and Tony Selmersheim displayed in Brussels (see Pl. *40*) showed the abundant promise about to be fulfilled.

Charpentier's exhibit at the 1900 Exposition Universelle included a dining-room commissioned by the Magasins du Louvre. His versatility was immediately evident. He designed not only the furniture, but also a silver wine cooler and carafe, embroidered table linen, and sculpted murals of *La Chasse*, *Vendange* and *Moisson*, flanking the central chimney on which was placed a large mantel clock. The effect was light and lively. Later that year the critic Jean Vignaud pinpointed Charpentier's primary talent, when he wrote, in discussing his teak *porte-manteau* and chairs at *Les Six*, 'one senses, above all, the vigorous talent of a sculptor in Alexandre Charpentier's furniture'.

Charpentier's exhibit at the 1901 Société Nationale des Beaux-Arts included his best-known work: the *meuble à quatuor à cordes* now in the Musée des Arts Décoratifs in Paris. Lined in Hungarian ash, the piece was pure Art Nouveau with a sumptuous organic frame enclosing bas-relief panels of *Le Violon*, *La Contrebasse* and two of *Danseuses*. The matching pair of music-stands were carved as the sweeping folds of a woman's dress, a familiar Charpentier theme. Compared to Carabin's upright piano – replete with nudes, cats and flowers – which was displayed simultaneously at the Société Nationale des Artistes français, Charpentier's use of furniture as a sculptural medium was considered well within the bounds of reason, while Carabin's was well beyond! Later that year, though, Charpentier's fireplace in *buis*, with floral marquetry by Alphonse Hérold, at *L'Art dans Tout* was criticized by Dampt for its injudicious choice of woods.

In 1902 Charpentier collaborated in two *ensembles* at the Société Nationale. The first, a billiard room for a house on Lake Geneva, was done in partnership with Bracquemond and Jules Chéret. Bracquemond's sculpted white wall panelling (executed by Buzin) and Chéret's charming pastels of the Four

Seasons provided a *de luxe* setting for Charpentier's billiard table, chairs, lamps, and enamelled silver coupe (executed by Falise). A door opened to the art gallery commissioned by the Baron Vitta to house his collection. Charpentier designed a pair of vitrines lightly carved with orchid sprays and a piano with a broad frieze of gambolling nudes painted by Albert Besnard. The critics were delighted.

Edouard Colonna

A designer of remarkable versatility, Colonna jumped from jewelry to porcelain tableware to furniture at will, bringing to each an abundant talent and delicacy of hand. Born in Mülheim-am-Rhein on 27 May 1862, Colonna studied architecture in Brussels before moving to the United States in 1882. After a sojourn in New York with Associated Artists (under Tiffany's directorship), he settled in Dayton, Ohio, designing railroad cars for the Barney & Smith Manufacturing Company. A short stay in Canada preceded his return to Europe where, from 1898 to 1903, he worked in Paris for Samuel Bing, designing items not only for the latter's gallery, but for the 1900 and 1902 Expositions Universelles. When Bing closed his gallery, Colonna travelled through Europe before returning to New York to work as an antique dealer and interior designer. In 1923, he moved south, settling on the Riviera, where he died on 14 October 1948, in Nice.

Colonna's contribution to Bing's pavilion at the 1900 Exposition Universelle was the drawing room, described in *The Studio* as 'A French Salon in the fullest sense of the word, the room in which we receive our guests, not the room in which we live . . . yet one longs to live there, so fascinating, so comfortable is its appearance.' The furniture, including a settee, chairs, tables, upright piano, carpets and music cabinet, was in orangewood, upholstered in yellow and green velours which matched the tones in the room's plush wall-hangings. A decorative fillip was provided by randomly placed Tiffany kerosene lamps and a vitrine crammed with Favrile flowerform and peacock vases. The effect was warm and feminine, totally in keeping with the rest of the pavilion.

Colonna's furniture designs at times bore a close resemblance to those of Gaillard and de Feure, a fact that is not surprising in view of the trio's close working relationship at Bing's. Unfortunately, none of them signed their pieces with regularity, if at all. This has created serious identification problems for today's collector. Colonna's furniture is, however, generally lighter, if not frailer, than that of the other two. He also applied symmetrical floral veneers on occasion to his more ambitious pieces, such as the music cabinet displayed in Turin. An undated suite of dressing-room furniture, with novel curved backs which extend beneath the cushioned seat almost to the floor, showed Colonna's participation in the epoch's search for something new.

Paul Croix-Marie

Paul Croix-Marie designed furniture in Paris in the early years of the twentieth century. In 1901 his tea-table at the Société Nationale des Artistes showed the innovation and strength of his designs; the splayed legs had angular knees beneath capitals carved with giant insect's eyes. Three years later, at the Salon des Arts Décoratifs, his suite of lounge furniture was shown with stencilled wallpaper by Bourgeot; the critics found the latter overpowering. The mirror, wall *étagères*, table and chair incorporated the same basic insect motifs. Everything had a pronounced Art Nouveau concept with sweeping curves heightened with carved brackets and friezes.

A year later at the Salon des Artistes français, Croix-Marie displayed a young woman's bedroom and a dining-room. The boldness was noticeably absent – in its place a very pleasant suite of furniture of gently Art Nouveau persuasion.

Damon & Colin

The Faubourg St Antoine was the centre for most of the Parisian cabinetmakers at the turn of the century, such as Pérol, Gouffé, Mercier, the Maison Kriéger, and Damon & Colin. The latter, often working in conjunction with Kriéger, were manufacturers of an entire range of period furniture. Their Art Nouveau *ensembles* were marketed under the category of 'Le Meuble Moderne'. These proved popular, particularly at the 1900 Exposition Universelle where examples of their work were acquired by the Christiania (Oslo), Hamburg, and St Gall Industrial Arts Museums. Exhibited were a dining-room and smoking-room. The elementary architectural shapes of the pieces were enhanced with rich upholstery and copper mounts to provide a sumptuous effect which belied their inexpensiveness. The dining-room was further decorated with a panelled oak wainscot, extending to three-fifths of the room's height, which was inlaid with floral marquetry to match the motifs on the furniture. The upper wall was covered with stencilled wallpaper to complete the overall effect of warmth and charm.

In 1902 Damon & Colin, in collaboration with Kriéger, displayed a salon/library at both the Salon des Industries du Mobilier at the Grand-Palais and at the Société Nationale. A year later their two library cabinets at the Salon incorporated large upper enclosed shelves with spire finials above twin cupboard doors set with heavy copper foliate mounts and hinges similar to the decoration used at the time by Rapin and Bellery-Desfontaines in their provincial-style furniture.

Jean-Auguste Dampt

Born at Venaray on the Côte d'Or in 1854, Dampt attended the Schools of Fine Arts in both Dijon and Paris before making his debut at the Salon in 1876. He was therefore a generation older than most Art Nouveau exponents and was able to provide valuable instruction to designers such as Charpentier and Angst.

Primarily a sculptor, he produced a wide range of objects including jewelry, medals and a silver series of orchid chandeliers and wall sconces marketed with huge success by M. Henri Beau at the 1900 Exposition Universelle. His furniture models were equally innovative but, as he himself handcrafted each with painstaking care, few in number.

Dampt's training was traditional. Sculpture such as his *La Fée Melusine et Le Chevalier Raymondin* in 1894 draws both its sentiment and its strength from the thirteenth century. Other works in wood are Renaissance in inspiration. It is startling, therefore, that he was drawn to the Art Nouveau challenge, if only briefly.

A founding member of *Les Cinq* society which exhibited at the Galerie des Artistes in 1897, he displayed a combination bookcase, vitrine and filing cabinet for engravings in oak interlaced with violet-tinted pinewood panels. The following year, his child's chair at the Salon of the Champ-de-Mars showed great charm and creativity. Entirely handmade by Dampt, the openwork triangular back incorporated a central panel with the word *AMA* entwined with mistletoe inlaid with mother-of-pearl berries. The apex was carved in full relief with two children.

Dampt's double bed at the Salon two years later showed his reluctance to relinquish fully his traditionalism for the tenets of Art Nouveau. The headboard with its high pediment and straight sides was strictly medieval in inspiration; its carved decoration pure Belle Epoque. The central three panels depicted allegorical figures of childhood, love, and learning beneath a frieze of female masks and the Gothic inspiration – *A songe d'or – cestuy qui doit – sans un remord*. The footboard was similarly sculptured in bas-relief with flowers and scrolls. In 1900 he exhibited a secretary at *L'Art dans Tout*. In 1901, again at the *L'Art dans Tout* exhibition, Dampt displayed a desk chair in cherrywood veneered in amaranth and lemonwood with cyclamen sprays. It, too, was refreshingly different. The side stretchers extended beneath and beyond the front legs to carved paw feet.

In 1906 another chair with fan-shaped crest and leather upholstery was favourably reviewed in *Art et Décoration*. No further reference to Dampt appeared after that date, suggesting that he may have retired soon thereafter. He died in 1946.

Georges de Feure

After 10 years as a largely unsung artist and interior designer, de Feure became an overnight sensation at the 1900 Exposition Universelle. Bing never disclosed the magic formula with which he fired the latent genius in the designers whom he invited to contribute to his gallery, but it clearly worked. De Feure had displayed with only moderate success a wide range of oils, watercolours, gouaches and pastels at the Champs de Mars since 1890 and, from 1896, a selection of furniture and objects, before joining Bing six months prior to the Exposition. Although Dutch-born, de Feure's taste was hailed as quintessentially French – light, refined and supremely delicate.

Bing's pavilion catapulted de Feure to international fame. The two rooms which he presented – a dressing-room and boudoir – were described in *L'Art Décoratif* by Gustave Soulier as 'irresistibly seductive, a decisive step along the way for modern furniture, a rallying point for future research'.

The dressing-room included a washstand, dressing table, *chaise longue*, chairs, screen, and cupboards in ash with burled Hungarian ash panelling. The cloth chair-covers were embroidered by Mrs Anaïs Fabre with grey, blue and mauve flowers and arabesques, the colours repeating themselves in the room's Japanese silk curtains, brocade wall hangings, and wool carpets. The key plates on the furniture, as a further refinement, were in grey nickelled iron. The effect, everyone agreed, was 'deliciously feminine'. A short corridor led to the boudoir. Here all the furniture was in giltwood upholstered in damask. Further wall hangings surrounded a white marble fireplace and a set of leaded glass panels depicting four of de Feure's Belle Epoque *femmes damnées*. Gabriel Mourey wrote of the boudoir in *The Studio*, 'I have no hesitation in saying, this is the thing that pleases me most; I declare this to be the pick of the entire building.'

The 1900 aftermath proved anti-climactic. De Feure continued to design for Bing and to exhibit at the annual Salons of the Société Nationale des Beaux-Arts, but the public were never again seduced to the same degree. In 1901 he showed a large walnut library bookcase, desk, chair upholstered in velours, bookcase with fabric curtains, vitrine, and corner console (the last two-mentioned are now in the Musée des Arts Décoratifs, Paris), together with a selection of porcelain tableware and *bonbonnières*. Francis Jourdain criticized him mildly for the inharmony of it all.

De Feure participated in the 1908 furniture Salon organized by the Chambre Syndicate de l'Ameublement. Included were a charming silvered-bronze and crystal wall sconce, curtains, a walnut buffet and an orangewood chest decorated with marquetry panels of peasant women. A contemporary magazine article notes that everything was commissioned by the Maison Kriéger, the manufacturer through whom de Feure marketed his designs after Bing's shop closed. Another suite of furniture, lightly carved with roses, bellflowers and berried ash, recalled the halcyon days of 1900.

De Feure continued to work commercially until World War I, after which he took up a professorship at the National School of Fine Arts in Paris.

Diot

A great deal of unsigned Art Nouveau furniture offered annually at auction in Paris, Versailles and Enghien is attributed to the firm of Diot. In many instances such attribution is incorrect despite the fact that the Maison Diot manufactured a large selection of such furniture at the turn of the century.

An undated sales catalogue (c. 1905) lists the firm's two locations: a salesroom at 23 rue Saint-Augustin and a studio on rue Chaligny. Illustrated are a range of *ensembles*, with pieces listed individually by price. The designs are well conceived and charming and in large part combining distinct Gaillard, Vallin, and Selmersheim contours and motifs. Most of the pieces incorporate lightly carved floral cartouches within sweeping curves; on occasion, Hungarian ash panelling was used to provide variation or, as in one *bureau plat*, a marquetry frieze of poppies. A choice of walnut or Cuban mahogany could be supplied. Bedrooms were offered in the following themes: holly, plane tree, poppy, and thorn-apple; libraries in pine, chestnut, and ginkgo; salons in rhododendron, Christmas rose, and eglantine.

Eugène Gaillard

A barrister by profession, Gaillard forsook the bar after ten years for a career as a designer/decorator. An early introduction to Samuel Bing established his career: he was the first to be hired for Bing's Maison Art Nouveau, being joined shortly by Georges de Feure and Edouard Colonna. Although the thrust of Gaillard's work – for which he is almost exclusively now known – was on furniture, he designed a wide range, including carpets and light fixtures.

Gaillard's legal background is evident in the logic with which he approached furniture design: the interrelationship of the various parts is always carefully conceived and seldom less than perfect. His preoccupation was with the outer, or enveloping, line by which a piece was unified.

The 1900 Exposition Universelle provided Gaillard with his first major opportunity, one which established him overnight as a foremost disciple of the modern movement. Bing entrusted the designs for the seven rooms in his pavilion on the Esplanade des Invalides at the Exposition to his proven trio: Gaillard, de Feure and Colonna. To Gaillard were assigned the vestibule, dining-room, and bedroom, three rooms with entirely different moods to test his versatility. For the vestibule Gaillard used *pochoir* drapes and a mosaic floor to offset a polished walnut *porte-manteau* and settee with mirrored back and shelves. The dining-room, furnished throughout in walnut carved with scrolled leaf ornamentation, included a panelled wainscot beneath a mural painted by the young Spanish artist, José-Maria Sert. The critics were hesitant in their praise, suggesting that the brightly painted walls overpowered the great charm and vigour of the *ensemble*. The bedroom, however, was beyond dispute. The bed, in pearwood with ash panelling and a mignonette-green silk coverlet, was elegance personified. The critic Gabriel Mourey, in summing up in *The Studio*, wrote 'Everything in this room is soft, delicate and carressing, without, however, any eccentricity or weakness. And in these days, when extravagance and over-elaboration are common, these are points deserving of unreasoned appreciation.'

The following year Gaillard displayed a pearwood table and *étagère* at the Salon Nationale. Both incorporated a deeply moulded exterior line which curved back sharply on itself at the corners. In 1902 a bookcase took the theme further: the same moulded contours on the cornice terminated at the angles in carved leaves above similarly sculpted door panels and ormolu pulls. Gaillard did not deviate from this theme for several years. A buffet and vitrine, shown in collaboration with Mangeant, at the 1903 Salon were identical. His teak dining-room at the 1906 Société des Artistes Décorateurs provided more of the same: the bold plant-like sweep in the sideboard repeated itself in the table and chairs, the latter upholstered in leather embossed with mimosa. Other pieces exhibited were a mahogany *sellette*, palisander music-stand, oak music cabinet and a walnut tea-table, the last a variation on the well-known model, introduced by Gaillard in 1902, with a top shelf above four hinged vertical trays which dropped outwards to form lower flanking shelves.

By 1907 Gaillard had simplified his designs significantly. A library cabinet at the Salon Nationale was rectangular except for flaring pad feet. Also shown was a walnut buffet with burl walnut panels. Again, the design was uninspired, signalling the post-1900 transitional period which was now beginning.

Mathieu Gallerey
Despite his admiration for Majorelle's cabinetry, Gallerey was careful not to try to emulate him. Few could achieve such perfection and fewer still could afford to purchase it. Gallerey saw clearly that the road to commercial success lay on a lower, more pragmatic, plane. Profitability lay in the machine and in industrial production. Gallerey's exhibit at the 1904 Société des Arts Décoratifs included *repoussé* copper panels of sunflowers and a buffet and chairs that 'could be made almost entirely by machine.' More important, they were entirely affordable; bold classical forms with lightly moulded floral decoration.

A year later, Gallerey participated in the competition of Mobiliers pour Habitations à bon marché at the Grand-Palais. The forty-two entrants – including Lambert, the Munich United Studios, and the Prague School of Decorative Arts – were invited to design a bedroom ensemble (double bed, *armoire*, night table, and two chairs) for a room of 12 m² with a ceiling height of 2.7 m. The maximum price of the suite could be 400 francs. Gallerey's exhibit, in wild cherry, generated high praise from Roger de Félice, who wrote that its simplicity, robustness and logical construction, all carefully planned to capabilities, made Gallerey 'the legitimate successor of bygone cabinetmakers'. In 1906, he exhibited an elegant bronze-mounted oak hall-tree at the Société Nationale and a dining-room in bleached oak at the Société des Arts Décoratifs. The chairs were upholstered in tooled leather and the buffet set with *repoussé* copper panels and machine-carved ginkgo leaf decoration. Again, Gallerey was praised for his unpretentious creativity. A year later he showed a bed and *armoire* in lemonwood, once more using the ginkgo fruit as his decorative theme.

Gallerey continued to produce his moderately priced furniture for several years, receiving praise in a 1909 article on furniture by Carabin. In 1910 he showed a wide selection of oak pieces at the Salon d'Automne in a neighbouring display to Gauthier and Neiss of Nancy.

Hector Guimard

Guimard's earliest recorded commission did not foretell the notoriety he achieved three short years later. In 1893 he designed the lettering and street numbers, executed in ceramics for him by Emile Muller in his Ivry pottery works, for the Hôtel Jassedé Villa de la Réunion at 142 avenue de Versailles, Paris. A meeting with Horta the following year clearly had a profound influence on his search for a new architectural idiom. The Castel Béranger at 14 rue La Fontaine, which he designed and built between 1895 and 1896, shook the architectural establishment to its foundations.

It was not so much that Guimard had introduced a highly controversial style – the need for something new, even iconoclastic, preoccupied architects in the 1890s – but that he flaunted his self-confidence at his antagonists, and there were soon many. Guimard's defiance revealed itself as bravado. He then annoyed his critics further by describing himself on his business cards as a (by which he clearly meant *the*) 'Architect of Art', to emphasize that he designed not only buildings but everything within them.

The Castel Béranger scandalized the French capital. Yet both Emile Molinier, a retired furniture conservator at the Louvre, and Guillaume Janneau, the renowned art historian writing in *Meubles et Décors*, sought its redeeming factors. Both saw Viollet-le-Duc's influence in the house's whiplash contours.

Molinier analysed Guimard's rejection of the straight line, except where essential for constructional purposes, and its replacement by 'curves, parabolas, and counter curves, all entwined, one within the other' as an attempt to evoke nature. He warned, though, that the new style would be short-lived if it were neither logical nor evolved from its immediate predecessor. The laws of evolution, in art as in all life, had to be upheld. Janneau pointed out, in defending the excesses of Guimard's furniture, that a great amount of it was built-in, hence its stylistic need to match the house's architecture. Pieces had to be seen in their original setting to be properly understood.

Francis Jourdain, in an 1899 article in *La Revue d'Art*, stood alone in his unconditional support of Guimard – 'Among the courageous few who have braved sarcasm, hatred, low vengeance and who have valiantly enrolled under the banner of the new art, one must cite M. Guimard, whose first experiments I have followed with a slightly egotistical interest as his need for independence pleases my own convictions most dearly . . .'

Guimard's furniture designs, even after the exposure afforded by several recent exhibitions – for example, in 1970 at The Museum of Modern Art, New York, and in 1971 at the Musée des Arts Décoratifs, Paris – still generate astonishment. Guimard based his designs on a plant's stem rather than on its flower, as did the School of Nancy. The resulting long sinuous lines intersected at intervals by knopped or knobbly protrusions – presumably the stylized joints from which offshoots emerge – appear tortuous and gnarled. These are more pronounced on smaller pieces such as *étagères*, plant stands, and tea-tables in the Castel Béranger. His chairs, superbly rendered in pearwood with leather or cloth upholstery, carry the theme to its ultimate.

Most of Guimard's furniture was produced in his own atelier. He selected fruit-woods, especially pear, for most of his furniture, although switching infrequently to walnut, palisander, green ebony, *jarrah*, citron, gaboon, and teak. The quality of cabinetmaking and carving is always superlative, to the point, even, that Guimard was criticized for the expense incurred in such intricacy, placing his work beyond the average home-owner's pocket. Other pieces were commissioned: for example, porcelain umbrella-stands and vases from the Sèvres Manufactory, glass doors from Trézel, and bronze photograph frames from Philippon.

In 1900 Guimard completed his blueprints for the entrances to the Paris Métro and the music hall Humbert de Romans. Houses for which, in most instances, he designed the furnishings included the Maison Coilliot in Lille, the Castel Henriette, his own villa in Vaucresson, the Hôtel Nozal, the Castel Val in Chaponval, and the Hôtel Mezzara at 60 rue La Fontaine. One of his last undertakings, from 1909 to 1913, was his own house at 122 avenue Mozart in

Paris. His widow donated a selection of pieces from some of the above to The Museum of Modern Art, New York, in 1949, and later to the Musée des Beaux-Arts in Lyons.

Louis Alphonse Hérold

Hérold participated at the Salon of *L'Art dans Tout* in the rue Caumartin for many years, showing his furniture alongside the works of Dampt, Charpentier, Plumet, and Moreau-Nélaton. Although his appearances were infrequent, Hérold maintained a high standard, being praised in 1899 by a critic for going to the countryside around Paris to regenerate his inspiration in the spontaneity and simplicity of nature. His hanging bookcase and *meuble pour albums* (album cabinet) bore out this philosophy: rectangular shapes lightly decorated with marquetry panels of dragonflies and prunus showed his conservatism. In 1900 and 1901 he displayed similar inlaid oak coffrets and an *armoire*, and the following year a table and inlaid cartonnier at the Société Nationale des Beaux-Arts.

At the 1903 Salon, Hérold's minister's-desk incorporated a rectangular frame raised on splayed feet; his earlier proclivity for marquetry had gone. By 1906 his furniture showed what in retrospect can be called a transitional style: his acacia and citron bedroom at the Société Nationale was devoid of decoration, relying on floral coverlets, curtains and *pochoir* wallpaper to provide a light decorative touch.

Théodore Lambert

Lambert was an architect who turned his attention to furniture in the late 1890s. His early work was eclectic, drawing its inspiration from Japanese, Empire and Pompeian furniture designs. Soon, however, his own characteristic, rather severe, style began to evolve. In 1901 at the Société Nationale des Beaux-Arts, he exhibited a chest of drawers, two settees and an *étagère* in lacquered wood with copper mounts. All were almost haunting in their sobriety, reminding one critic of a funeral parlour and another of the worst elements of the Empire style – its stiffness and dryness.

The next year saw a softening of both this severity and its censure. The starkness of a pair of tubular copper beds was offset by elaborate scrollwork in the head- and footboards suggesting to one enthusiastic critic that they must have been designed for a seaside villa. The matching copper wall-shelf at the Société des Arts Décoratifs emphasized Lambert's fondness for metal as the medium with which to stress the modernity of his designs; though he continued to produce wooden furniture until World War I, he clearly saw the select range of metal pieces which he introduced intermittently from 1903 as a step towards the future era of mass production.

In 1905, his participation in the competition Mobiliers pour Habitations a bon marché was clearly inspired by his awareness that machine-made furniture, whether of wood or metal, would soon be an inevitability. Later that year at the Salon Nationale, he showed samples of the interior commissioned by a M. Krug for his house in Rheims. Of particular interest were the silk curtains and wall-papers whose warm orange and yellow tones softened the starkness of the furniture. At the 1906 Société des Arts Décoratifs, Lambert exhibited a collector's cabinet – 'for inro, tzubas or netsuke' – in varnished mahogany applied with copper mounts. The design of the piece was, most suitably, Japanese. A matching settee and fauteuil were upholstered in embroidered velours. His most charming exhibit was a small mahogany games-table inset with a stained leather playing surface by Mlle Germain. A year later, his bed-room at the Société Nationale des Beaux-Arts included a corner bookcase, chimney and *armoire* in polished lemonwood. The main influence was again Oriental, with delicate brass furniture mounts cast as peonies and chry-santhemums.

Lambert continued to exhibit for many years, receiving favourable reviews for what the critics determined as his greatest asset, his spirit of reason. G. Janneau hailed him as one of the masters of the period who, like Sorel, emerged to bring about an orderly transition from the exuberance of 'the Gallés, the Majorelles and the Plumets' to a style more in keeping with the sombre mood of the world of 1910.

Abel Landry

On completion of his studies at the Limoges School of Decorative Arts, Landry transferred to the School of Beaux-Arts in Paris to become an architect. An early decision to collaborate with an industrial designer paved the way to Landry's later preoccupation with the interiors of the houses which he designed. Like Tony Selmersheim, Henri Sauvage, and Henri Provensal, Landry became better known finally in the decorative arts than in his chosen profession.

By the late 1890s Landry was well established as an architect, having com-pleted commissions for several houses and villas near Paris, artists' studios in Bordeaux, and hotels in Lyons and Marseilles. The invitation by the critic Julius Meier-Graefe to design his new art gallery, La Maison Moderne, drew Landry into the mainstream of the Art Nouveau movement. In collaboration with the other designers whom Meier-Graefe had commissioned to produce items for the gallery – in particular, Paul Follot, Maurice Dufrêne and Henry van de Velde – Landry was soon likewise in pursuit of the epoch's 'new' rationality. In 1900 he displayed a study for a M. Cahen in which the Art Nouveau influence was clearly visible: the characteristic whiplash motifs on the pedestal desk and settee were repeated in the room's wallpaper and stained-glass windows. The following year Landry displayed a wide range of furniture at La Maison Moderne including complete dining-room, library, and bedroom *ensembles*. The critics were impressed; while certain pieces were judged to be too massive, Landry showed an exciting creativity in a secretary and dressing-table. His selection of chairs, upholstered in velours with applied leather flowers, was likewise successful, as was a macassar ebony screen with opalescent leaded-glass panels.

In 1903 the critic Emile Sedeyn's long article in *L'Art Décoratif* on Landry's most recent commissions – a dentist's consulting room in the Madeleine and a bachelor's apartment off the Champs-Elysées – pointed to his versatility. A library, designed in collaboration with the architect Augustin Rey, at the Société des Artistes français later that year was, however, too eclectic for the critics' taste. Its hybrid of neoclassical and Egyptian influences was deplored as theatrical and retrogressive.

When La Maison Moderne closed in 1905 Landry had to commission various Paris studios and retailers to make and sell his designs. His furniture, for example, was manufactured by La Maison Lucas and sold by Camille Garnier; porcelain tableware was marketed by Louriaux; silk screens by Ballauf et Petitpont; lamps by Déroullia and Petit. By 1907 the Art Nouveau influence was largely gone from his designs, replaced by unpretentious logic and elegance.

Georges Nowak
Nowak worked in Paris at the turn of the century, exhibiting intermittently at the Société des Artistes français. The size and structure of his furniture are reminiscent of those of Vallin, although he catered to a more modest budget. Large, heavily moulded pieces were lightly carved with stylized flowers, often with a quiet elegance that drew praise from the critics. Most of his pieces appear too massive, however. A buffet displayed in 1903 has a provincial sturdiness that disguises its Art Nouveau inspiration. Similarly, a dining table exhibited in the same year has four robust tree-form legs linked to a huge central trunk-like column by four curved stretchers that provide both an unnecessary amount of support and an overplayed visual effect. His lady's desk was much better rendered: light marquetry and ormolu mounts effectively enhance the piece. A side-chair, introduced two years later, had unusual pierced side brackets running from beneath the front of the seat to the feet of the rear legs. The concept was clearly in fashion; identical models by Louis Majorelle and Abel Landry appeared at the same Salon.

Nowak apparently did not sign his furniture, which creates enormous difficulties of authentication today.

Charles Plumet and Anthony Selmersheim

Charles Plumet and his student, Anthony Selmersheim, became in the 1890s what Francis Jourdain later described as 'the inseparable collaborators and Siamese twins of success.' Both were architects whose work expanded to include designs for entire interiors. Plumet was the senior partner. His façades and furnishings for houses on the boulevard des Italiens, avenue Bois-de-Boulogne, and rue de Tocqueville received generous coverage in contemporary art reviews. Tony Selmersheim was considered his protégé, one whose contributions included a special talent for metal and crystal light fixtures. Gabriel Mourey, commenting in *The Studio* on Selmersheim's display at *Les Six* in 1898, wrote, 'He has great and original talent, and as he is on the right road, all that remains for him is to go straight ahead, and then we may count on having a supply of beautiful works of applied art.'

The aspects of Plumet and Selmersheim's furniture which pleased everyone – on reading through contemporary literature it is extraordinary to find that *nobody* appears to have found fault with any aspect of their work – were the irreproachable proportions and quiet elegance of their designs. They showed a wide range of *ensembles* at both the annual *L'Art dans Tout* exhibitions and the Société Nationale des Beaux-Arts. Their furniture – in rosewood, padouck, oak or ash – was invariably displayed in rooms in which Plumet juxtaposed his wide selection of wall decorations – embroidered damasks, *pochoirs*, wood panelling, tapestries, and, above connecting doors, stained-glass transoms. Several pieces of furniture were charming in their ingenuity; in particular the combination hall settee/*porte-manteau* which condensed a seat, bookcase, desk and umbrella-rack into a compact unit to be fitted into the semicircular foot of a spiral staircase.

Another innovative piece was the ash *chaise longue* which Selmersheim exhibited at the 1901 Salon. It was fitted with a raised back which incorporated a mirror above drawers and shelves. A year earlier, their display at the Exposition Universelle included a foyer and bedroom in walnut and padouck. Works commissioned from other artists completed the two ensembles: a faience cartel clock by Barbedienne; sconces by Schneck; ceramics by Muller; and a frieze by Jourdain. On other occasions, Charles Guérin provided painted panels and Félix Aubert, a co-member of *L'Art dans Tout*, several friezes.

By 1905, the emphasis had shifted to inexpensive furniture to cater to the newly evolving middle-class budget. The bold moulded sweep of their earlier designs more or less disappeared; a restrained machine-made adaptation was substituted. Furniture in Caledonian walnut was inlaid with copper embossed with eglantines. In 1906 they exhibited an oak dining-room *for fixed-income buyers* at the Société Nationale des Beaux-Arts. By 1910 the Art Nouveau thrust of their work had gone: pieces exhibited at the 1910 and 1911 Salons d'Automne were functional but uninspired.

As neither Plumet nor Selmersheim signed their furniture it is today extremely difficult to identify without crossreference to a contemporary photograph.

Raguel

Raguel was a minor Parisian cabinetmaker who exhibited in the early years of the twentieth century. His dining-room at the 1903 Salon d'Automne was intricate and refined, including a fireplace in bleached oak to match the table with its band of veneered grape leaves and hops. A year later, at the Salon des Artistes Décorateurs, he displayed a charming child's cot with a pierced rail above floral pewter inlay.

Raguel was described in *L'Art Décoratif* in 1905 by Roger de Félice as an interesting young artist. Certainly the bedroom suite of furniture which he showed was extremely innovative. The fluid sweeps of the contours were enhanced with tooled leather upholstery.

No reference to Raguel appears in decorative art reviews after 1907.

Henri Rapin

Rapin was an art professor who drew on Gothic furniture designs as the starting-point for his own models. Sturdy rectilinear structures, such as the cabinet which he displayed at the 1903 Salon, have a distinct fifteenth-century symmetry. To these, Rapid applied his own forms of decoration: *repoussé* copper panels, painted friezes and heavily hammered wrought-iron mounts and hinges. There is a French provincial and, at times, arts-and-crafts appearance to his pieces which inspired his student Bellery-Desfontaines to produce a similar range of furniture.

Rapin had a proclivity for large items – buffets, cabinets and *armoires* – which he showed frequently at the Salons. Two oak buffets, in 1909 and 1910, incorporated copper panels set within broad mounts carved with Belle Epoque maidens, raised on flaring tripod bases. The effect was charming.

Henri Sauvage (1873–1932)

Educated as an architect in his home town of Nancy, where he designed Louis Majorelle's villa, Sauvage moved to Paris in the 1890s to work both independently and in association with Charles Sarazin, a fellow architect. Sauvage's career parallels that of Plumet; both went beyond the blueprint of the building to its interior and furnishings. A lengthy article in *Art et Décoration* by Gustave Soulier in 1899 discussed Sauvage's diversity and the numerous artist/craftsmen whom he commissioned to produce his designs: silk friezes *au pochoir* by

Jolly; furniture by Kriéger, Page & Noël, or Peigné; bronze hinges and key plates by Carmus; earthenware by Bigot; wrought-iron by Regius; wallpaper by Francis Jourdain et Cousin; and others – Mlle Abbème, Laumonnerie, Achille Cesbron and even Sarah Bernhardt – whose specific contributions were unlisted. Initially considered too eclectic, his furniture soon achieved a certain unity and rationalism which pleased the critics. In 1899 Sauvage exhibited a table and chair at the second competition of the Union Centrale des Arts Décoratifs.

In 1900 he completed his designs for the Café de Paris and Loïe Fuller's theatre at the Exposition Universelle. He also displayed a chair and table at *L'Art dans Tout*, which he had recently joined.

At the Société Nationale des Beaux-Arts the following year, his display included a buffet, games-table and chair upholstered in grey velours. In 1903, in collaboration with Sarazin, he showed a bedroom which was heavily Art Nouveau in inspiration. Another commission, a bathroom for a M. Jansen, included ceramic tiles by Bigot, cupboards by Jourdain, and *pâte-de-verre* plaques of nymphs by Alexandre Charpentier. Soon to follow was an actress's changing-room tastefully furnished with a *chaise longue*, dressing table, screen, and chairs.

Pierre Selmersheim

Pierre Selmersheim had the misfortune to be Tony Selmersheim's younger brother. Although similarly versatile, he lacked the huge opportunities afforded by Tony's association with Charles Plumet, and therefore laboured for a long time to achieve his own identity. It must have frustrated him always to have had his work at the Salons reviewed in contemporary magazines *after* those of Plumet and his brother, almost as a postscript. Selmersheim did, however, have one article written exclusively on his work by Gustave Soulier in *L'Art Décoratif* in 1902. In it Soulier discussed an apartment which Selmersheim had recently completed 'to the specific needs and taste of the client'. The bedroom, library, and bathroom were respectively in walnut, Congolese padouck, and varnished ash, each wood carefully chosen to meet the mood and function of the room. The walls were hung with wallpaper by Jolly and Sauvage. Two delightful appurtenances were a bronze chandelier with floral glass shade in the dining-room and a stained-glass window, executed by Socard, in the bathroom. The furniture, with moulded curves enclosing vacant panels, was elegantly restrained, similar to, but less spirited than, Gaillard's designs at the time. Selmersheim's minister's desk and bookcase at the Société Nationale in the same year received favourable comment. Earlier, his ceramic fountain, executed by Muller, at the 1901 Salon had generated an uncharacteristically hostile comment from Soulier, who wrote 'his fountain is of purely cerebral invention . . . detached from any living concept of nature . . . his metalware is much purer and refined . . . why does he not adhere to these qualities?'

Much more favourable was the critic Gerdeil's comment on the tea-table which Selmersheim displayed six months later: 'one of the rarest things one can see: a piece of furniture without precedent. It is a veritable windfall. . . .' The table, executed by Ausseur, represents today an Art Nouveau *tour de force*, incorporating the very best of the style's design philosophies with total functionalism.

In 1906, Selmersheim displayed his interior for a M. Dubufe at the Société Nationale and a stained-glass window, executed by Eugène Martin, at the Société des Artistes Décorateurs. He continued to exhibit until World War I, showing a set of dining-room seat furniture upholstered in interwoven leather straps at the 1913 Salon.

Louis Sorel

The noted critic Gustave Soulier devoted the lion's share of an article on furniture in *Art et Décoration* in 1898 to an analysis of Sorel's furniture designs. Sorel, Soulier felt, was one of the few to both comprehend and harness the machine's production possibilities, others being Bigaux and Le Coeur, Louis Bonnier, and the Belgian architect Paul Hankar.

Sorel was an architect who initially designed furniture only for his own houses. Later he showed a range of pieces at the annual Salons. His work was characteristic of the machine-made furniture of the period, lacking the ornateness of most of his contemporaries. Sturdy, gently curved structures have at times an almost rudimentary and Gothic appearance. Chairs and settees in bleached cherry or ash were decorated with fabrics by Félix Aubert. Examples, displayed in 1901 at the *L'Art dans Tout* and at the Société Nationale des Beaux-Arts, have a distinctly Art Nouveau appearance. In the same year a dessert and buffet brought praise for their sober elegance. Sorel reverted to medieval cabinetmaking techniques to construct his furniture, in this respect adopting Viollet-le-Duc's mid-nineteenth-century philosophies.

82 *Hestaux:* the étagère exhibited at the Société Nationale des Beaux-Arts in 1901. Entitled *La Nuit*, its theme was symbolic, including frogs, a winged nymph and insects.

83 *Prouvé:* panel in tooled and poly-chromed leather with bronze and copper mounts. Now in the Musée de l'Ecole de Nancy, it originally belonged to Eugène Vallin and was displayed at the 1903 Exposition of the Ecole de Nancy in Paris.

84 *Vallin:* the dining room exhibited at the Salon d'Automne in 1910.

85 *Vallin:* sculpted bedroom suite of furniture.

86 *Vallin:* the minister's desk and chair exhibited in the 1903 Exposition of the Ecole de Nancy and illustrated in *La Lorraine Artiste*, 1902, p. 27. It is now in the Musée de l'Ecole de Nancy.

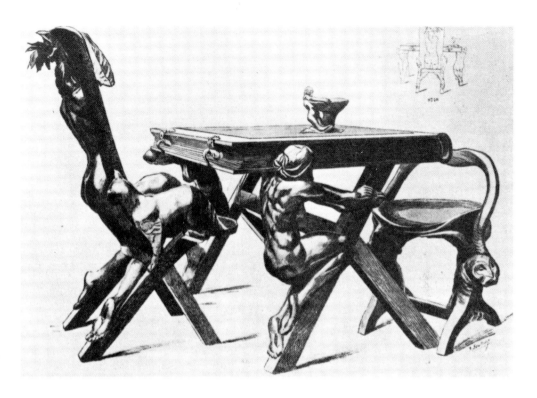

87 *Carabin:* the sketch for the walnut table, *fauteuil* and *chaise*, exhibited at the Société Nationale des Beaux-Arts, 1896. The mounts on the table are in wrought-iron. Illustrated in *La Revue d'Art*, 1900, p. 163.

88 *Carabin:* bookcase in pearwood, exhibited at the Société Nationale des Beaux-Arts in 1905.

89 *Carabin: coffre à bibelots* in sculpted oak with wrought-iron mounts, exhibited at the Société Nationale des Beaux-Arts in 1894. Illustrated in *Art et Industrie*, 1910.

90 *Angst:* dining room in walnut, exhibited at the Société Nationale des Beaux-Arts in 1905.

91 *Hamm:* dressing table shown at the Salon d'Automne in 1903.

92 *Gauthier:* marquetry cabinet with ormolu flowerform mounts, *c.* 1905.

93 *André:* a double bed in polished walnut shown at the 1903 Exposition of the Ecole de Nancy.

94 *André:* this tapestry loom was exhibited at both the 1903 Ecole de Nancy Exposition and the 1904 Salon of the *Société Lorraine des Amis des Arts.*

95 *Brunot:* Ferdinand Brunot (1862–1955), from Vosges, was a Professor of the French language at the Sorbonne who designed a dining room which included this elaborate buffet, now in the Musée de l'Ecole de Nancy.

96 *Ferez:* this marquetry screen was illustrated in *La Lorraine Illustrée* in both 1899 and 1901. The mahogany frame is carved with woodbine.

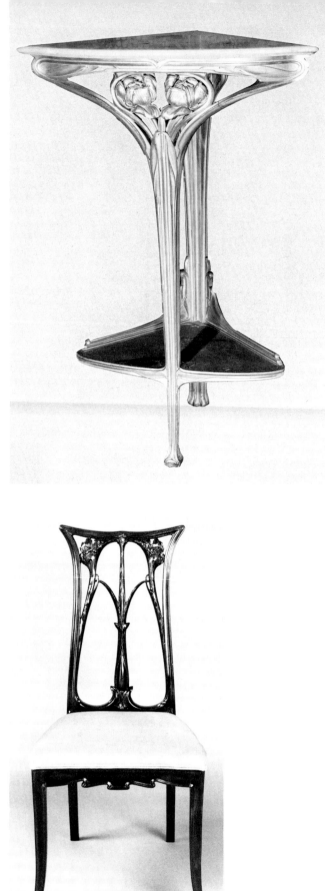

97 *de Feure:* three-leaf screen with embroidered silk panels. The model was included in de Feure's boudoir in Bing's Pavilion at the 1900 Exposition Universelle. Illustrated in *Art et Décoration*, January–June 1901, p. 84.

98 *de Feure:* corner giltwood console, now in the Musée des Arts Décoratifs, Paris. Illustrated in *Art et Décoration*, January–June 1901, p. 83.

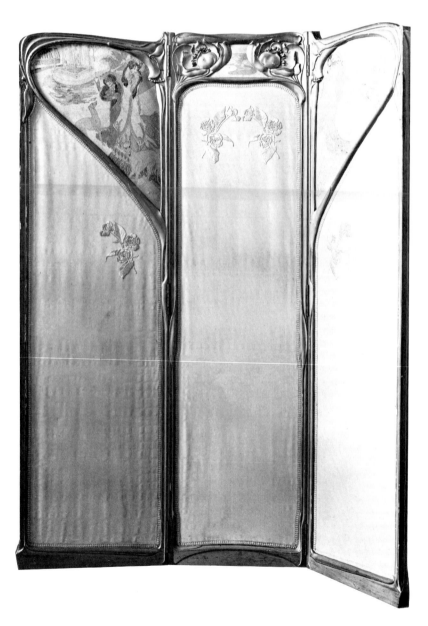

99 *de Feure:* a mahogany chair, *c.* 1900.

100 *de Feure*: a *canapé* exhibited in Bing's Pavilion at the 1900 Exposition Universelle. It is now in the Musée des Arts Décoratifs, Paris.

101 *Colonna*: tea table, *c.* 1900.

102 *Colonna*: a *chaise* upholstered in a peacock feather velours, part of Colonna's drawing room in Bing's Pavilion at the 1900 Exposition Universelle.

103 *Colonna*: a *fauteuil*, part of the same drawing room at Bing's Pavilion.

104 *Guimard:* chair with plush upholstery.

105 *Guimard:* side chair in pearwood with tooled leather upholstery.

106 *Guimard:* side table and upholstered stool, *c.* 1898.

107, 108 *Guimard:* two pearwood *bergères.*

109 *Guimard:* chair in pearwood.

110, 111 *Guimard:* a pearwood *chaise* and *fauteuil.*

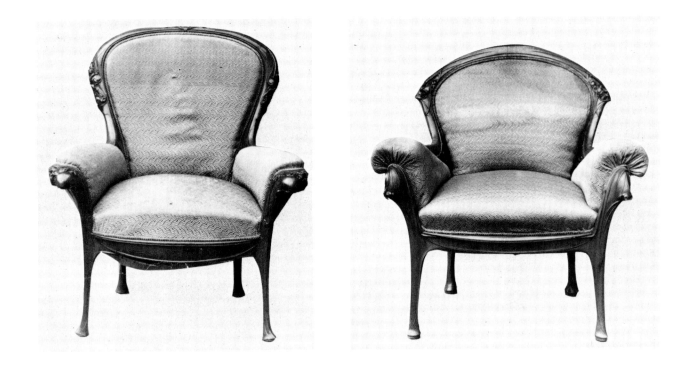

112 *Guimard:* oak longcase clock, 1910, for his own house at 122 avenue Mozart. It is now in the Musée des Arts Décoratifs, Paris.

113 *Guimard:* cupboard in pearwood, 1900, now in the Musée des Arts Décoratifs, Paris.

114 *Guimard:* African and olive ash desk. *Collection The Museum of Modern Art, New York.*

115 *Guimard:* double bed, night table and guéridon, pearwood, 1900.

116 *Guimard:* corner cabinet in pearwood.

117 *Charpentier:* ceramic fountain by Bigot for the dining-roon commissioned by Adrien Bénard for his villa, 1901.

118 *Charpentier:* view of the mahogany dining-room commissioned by Adrien Bénard in 1901.

119 *Guimard:* design for a fireplace, *c.* 1903, pencil, chalk, and charcoal on paper. Executed in lava with a central panel of glazed stoneware, the fireplace is still *in situ* in the Maison Coilliot, Lille.

120 *Guimard:* Fireplace surround in cast-iron.

121 *Guimard:* chimney over-mantel mirror in pearwood.

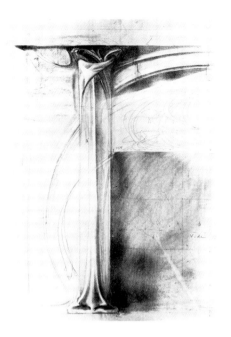

122 *Gaillard:* this sketch for a salon cabinet was illustrated in *Art et Décoration*, January–June 1902, p. 26.

123 *Gaillard:* a sketch for a vitrine illustrated in *Art et Décoration* January–June 1902, p. 25.

124 *Gaillard:* buffet in mahogany, 1900, now in the National Museum, Stockholm. A similar model was exhibited in Bing's Pavilion at the 1900 Exposition Universelle; see *La Revue des Arts Décoratifs*, 1900, p. 255.

125 *Gaillard:* cabinet in pearwood.

126 *Gaillard:* mahogany side chair, before 1900, said by the artist to be the first chair that he designed for Bing.

127 *Gaillard:* side chair, 1906, in rosewood with silk upholstery in the *pluie d'or* pattern, woven by Bouvard et Cie., Lyons. Now in the Musée des Arts Décoratifs, Paris.

128 *Gaillard:* chair with tooled leather upholstery.

129 *Belville:* upright piano in mahogany with tooled leather panelling, shown at the Société Nationale des Beaux-Arts, 1904.

130 *P. Selmersheim:* sketch for a bedroom, illustrated in *L'Art Décoratif,* 1902

131 *P. Selmersheim:* sketch for a dining-room ensemble, illustrated in *L'Art Décoratif,* 1902.

132 *P. Selmersheim:* mahogany tea-table, illustrated in *L'Art Décoratif* 1901, p. 38.

133 *T. Selmersheim:* Tea-table.

134 *Louis Brouhot:* marquetry cabinet shown at the Société Nationale des Beaux-Arts in 1904.

135 *T. Selmersheim : coiffeuse* with metal ornamentatio

136 *Benouville :* lady's writing desk.

137 *Sauvage :* marquetry tea-table.

138 *Benouville :* marquetry two-tier teatable.

139 *Hoentschel :* armchair in carved Algeria syca-more with leather upholstery. One of four chairs and a table for the Salon du Bois in the Pavilion of the Union Centrale des Arts Décoratifs at the 1900 Exposition Universelle. It is now in the Musée des Arts Décoratifs, Paris.

140 *Landry :* chair, 1901, designed for La Maison Moderne.

141 *Landry :* tea-table in pearwood with silvered bronze mounts, executed by Gillet & Barroux and shown at the Société des Artistes Français in 1904.

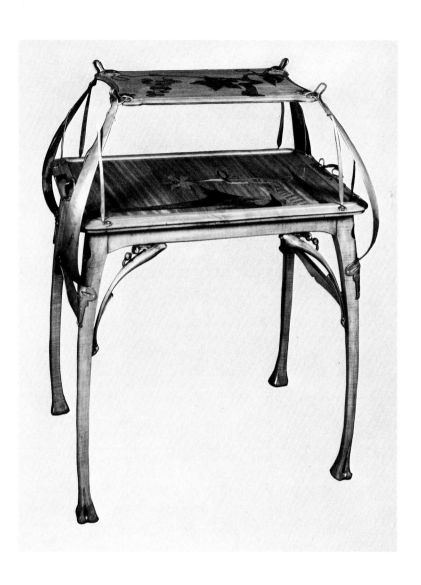

142 *Rapin:* buffet, *c.* 1903, with painted panels and wrought-iron key plates and hinges.

143 *Boverie:* buffet in walnut with bronze mounts, displayed at the Salon in 1902.

144 *Bellery-Desfontaines:* desk, part of a lady's bedroom in walnut shown at the Société Nationale des Beaux-Arts, 1907. The lamp has a wrought-iron mount by Szabo.

145 *Bellery-Desfontaines:* armoire in walnut, 1907.

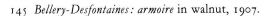

146 *Boverie:* lady's desk in lemonwood, shown at the Société des Arts Réunis at the Galerie Georges Petit, 1902. The applied mistletoe decoration is in bronze.

147 *Lambert:* A pair of brass beds, exhibited at the Société Nationale des Beaux-Arts in 1902. Illustrated in *L'Art Décoratif*, July–December 1902, p. 168.

148 *Croix-Marie:* buffet, *c.* 1903.

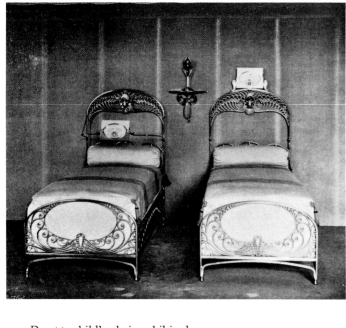

149 *Dampt:* child's chair exhibited at Les Six exhibition and illustrated in *Art et Décoration* January–June 1897, p. 74.

150 *Savine:* this extraordinary grand piano, in mahogany with bronze mounts, was designed by Léopold Savine for Pleyel-Wolf, Lyon et Cie., and displayed at the Société Nationale des Beaux-Arts, 1906.

151 *Diot* (attributed to): sideboard with *repoussé* brass panels.

152 *Horta:* wall mirror.

153 *Horta:* fruitwood chair in the Hôtel Solvay, Brussels, upholstered in velvet brocade, *c.* 1890.

154 *Horta:* billiard table.

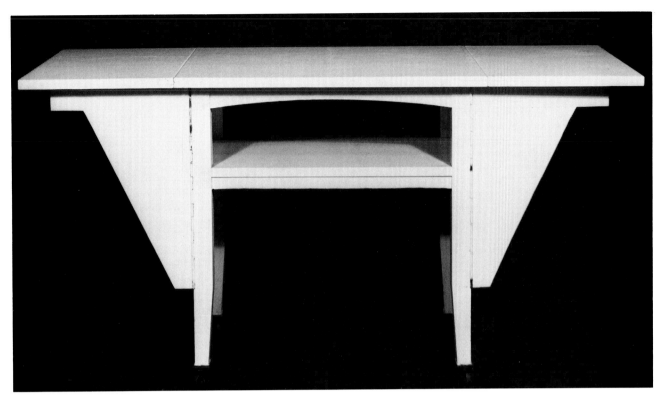

155, 156 *Van de Velde:* painted folding table.

157 *Van de Velde:* armchair.

158 *Serrurier-Bovy:* buffet, *c.* 1900.

159 *Serrurier-Bovy:* open armchair, showing the provincial style characteristic of his work.

160 *Endell:* armchair, 1899.

161 *Endell:* liquor cabinet, *c.* 1900. A similar model was exhibited at the Museum Villa Stuck, Munich, in 1977.

162 *Eckmann:* armchair, 1900.

163 *Riemerschmid:* armchair, 1903.

164 *Riemerschmid:* side chair, 1899, in oak with leather upholstery. Now in The Museum of Modern Art, New York.

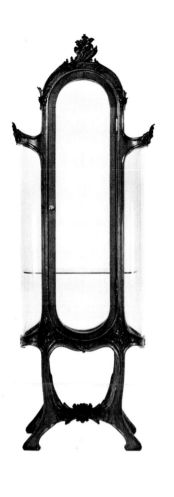

165 *Busquets:* large living-room vitrine.

166 *Carlo Zen:* desk, *c.* 1905; wood inlaid with mother-of-pearl and with ormolu mounts.

167 *Gaudí:* Oak bench, Casa Calvet, 1898–1904.

168 *Gaudí:* hand-carved oak pew with wrought-iron mounts for the Chapel of Colonial Güell, 1898–1915.

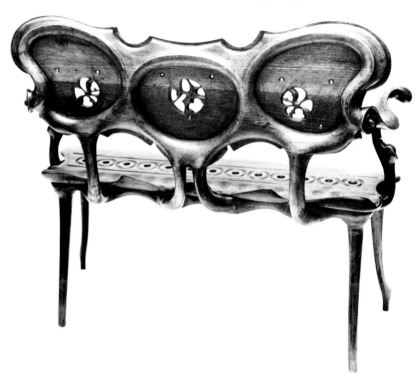

169 *Bugatti:* armchair, wood lined in vellum, with pewter and brass.

170 *Bugatti:* cupboard in wood lined in vellum, with pewter, brass and painted decoration. *c.* 1905.

171 *Mackintosh:* one of two white-painted oak armchairs for Mrs. Rowati's house at 14, Kingsborough Gardens, Glasgow, 1901–02. Mackintosh made a third one for himself and exhibited all three in Moscow in 1903.

172 *Behrens:* polished beech-wood dining chair, 1902.

173 *Hoffmann:* desk, *c.* 1901.

174 *Hoffmann:* mantel clock illustrated
in *Innen-dekoration* in 1902.

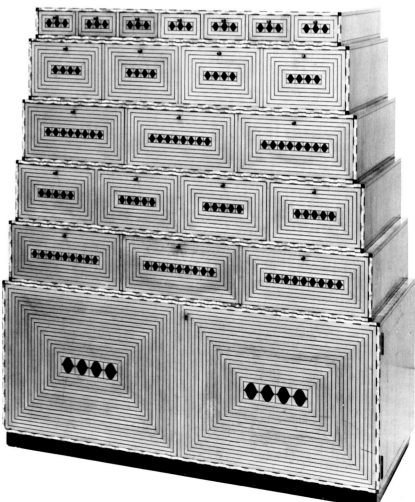

175 *Unger:* writing cabinet exhibited by the Vienna School of Decorative Arts as part of the Austrian display at the 1900 Exposition Universelle.

176 *Hoffmann:* chair in painted beechwood with red leather, 1903–06, manufactured by Jacob and Josef Kohn.

177 *Hoffmann:* chest of drawers in ebony, boxwood and mother-of-pearl, 1910–14. Manufactured by Niedermoser, Vienna.

178 *Mackintosh:* A sketch for the dining-room in a house for a connoisseur of the arts, part of Mackintosh's entry for a competition in the December 1900 issue of *Zeitschrift für Innendekoration*, published by Alexander Koch.

179 *Mackintosh:* The drawing room at 120 Mains Street, Glasgow, 1899/1900, designed for himself.

Belgium

Brussels was the crucible of the Art Nouveau movement in Europe. In furniture, its momentum was provided by the city's architects. As J.-G. Watelet wrote in *Discovering Antiques* in 1971, 'The main characteristic of Belgian furniture of this period is its architectural quality, which shows itself in two different ways. First of all, most of the furniture was designed to fit in with a particular architectural scheme and it does not often stand on its own merits ... second, furniture of this period can be called architectural because it is mainly the work of architects ...'

Three people predominated: Horta, van de Velde and Serrurier-Bovy. All designed total interiors (*Gesamtkunstwerk*) in harmony with their buildings.

Much credit must be given to the aesthete and critic Octave Maus, who formed the artistic group, *Les Vingt*, in 1884. Ten years later, as the Belgian Art Nouveau movement was reaching full bloom, the group expanded to become *La Libre Esthétique*, providing an international forum not only for resident artists but for all who aspired to the Art Nouveau idiom. At first composed of painters, sculptors, men of letters, and musicians, *Les Vingt* gradually opened its annual Salons to works of art, including furniture. Several Belgian architects participated; not only Horta, van de Velde and Serrurier-Bovy, but Paul Hankar, Georges Hobé, and Antoine Pompe. Others to display Art Nouveau furniture were Edouard de Grauw, a tapestry weaver who worked in collaboration with the interior designer, François König, and Georges Lemmen, the artist-turned-designer.

The Belgians appear to have boycotted the 1900 Exposition Universelle; only van de Velde was represented by his exhibits in Bing's pavilion. In 1902, at Turin, the furniture of Horta and Hobé was joined by examples by Govaerts and Sneyers.

Art Nouveau in Belgium was relatively short-lived. Following the successful Liège Exposition in 1905, the style was quickly moderated. Curves were reduced as objects grew calmer. No doubt the Secession's influence was felt when Hoffmann built the Palais Stoclet in 1905; soon Art Nouveau's leadership had shifted to Glasgow and Vienna.

Victor Horta

Born of a Ghent cobbler in 1861, Horta enrolled at the Brussels Academy in 1881. On receiving his diploma, he was interned by Alphonse Balat, the architect of the Royal Greenhouses at Laeken. Balat was a rigid traditionalist, so it is astonishing that Horta's radical spatial and structural concepts could have been nurtured to full bloom under such supervision.

Primarily a designer of residential architecture, Horta had first to persuade his clients that tradition must be abandoned, not only in the shape and decoration of the house, but in its furnishings. Gone was the safely proven formality of Flemish eighteenth- and nineteenth-century architecture; in its place he relied on subtle gradations of colour, metal arabesques, undulating woodwork and broad inroads of light.

Horta's creativity reached its zenith between 1893 and 1903, a decade during which he completed more than thirty major projects, beginning with the residence for the engineer Emile Tassel. Horta designed the Tassel house as two independent sections, the floors of which were staggered in height but linked by upper galleries. A continuous whiplash curve united all the building's elements, both architectural and decorative. This 'Horta line', as it immediately became known, was described by Robert L. Delevoy in 1971:

Here is the Horta line in mad exuberance . . . It whips across ground, walls, and ceiling, breaks out of capitals, runs down flights of stairs, spreads through the branches of the chandeliers, creeps across the window leading. It lashes around everywhere, wraps around, intertwines, unties itself, as flexible as a liana – a liana tamed however by geometry. Whether it developed with Mackintosh's line or preceded it, descended from Toorop or harkened back to the sources, this line was born in the ambience of the period. Still Horta gave it its special quality, made it split the air like a coachman's whip. Certainly the line alone did not create the 1900 style – but it was the style's fundamental theme.

The line repeated itself in the furniture, though never with the free reign afforded it in ceiling struts, column capitals and chandeliers. Horta's furniture designs for each client – Tassel, Frison, Solvay, van Eetvelde, Aubecq, etc. – were unique; each commission entailed new challenges requiring new solutions. None of his designs was made to be reproduced commercially. In 1897, *Art et Décoration* included an article on the interiors of his Château de la Hulpe and the house for Baron van Eetvelde, the Secretary of State for the Belgian Congo. In 1902, the same magazine covered both his dining-room with silver candlesticks by Fernand Dubois at the Turin Exhibition and the recently completed Hôtel Solvay on the avenue Louise in Brussels.

Horta's preferred furniture woods included mahogany, maple, and a selection of pale fruitwoods, often adorned with ormolu mounts. The upholstery was always sumptuous, well in keeping with his rich interiors. Blue and yellow brocaded silks or striped velvets matched the *pochoir* wallpapers in his drawing rooms and boudoirs. Unfortunately, a great many of Horta's houses were destroyed in the 1950s rush to tear down and rebuild central Brussels. Today, the few pieces of his furniture which reach the open market are eagerly contested by collectors.

Gustave-Nicolas-Joseph Serrurier-Bovy

The oldest of five children, Serrurier-Bovy was born on 27 July 1859 in Liège. His father, Louis Serrurier, was a furniture retailer who in 1866 purchased the bankrupt business of M. J.-J. Bovy, Gustave's future father-in-law. From 1874 Serrurier-Bovy studied at both the Athénée and the Académie des Beaux-Arts, qualifying as an architect in 1883. A trip to England the following year exposed him both to William Morris's philosophies and to a wide range of English decorating techniques and materials: wallpapers, carpets, wrought-iron, ceramics, and furniture. On his return, he established himself at 38 rue de l'Université in Liège.

Serrurier-Bovy concentrated initially on architecture. An early commission (in 1887) was for a university hospital. Others soon followed. It was only in 1894 that he displayed a *Chambre d'Artisan*, choosing the first Salon of *La Libre Esthétique* to launch his career as a decorator. The *ensemble* was characteristic of his later work; brightly coloured ceilings and walls offset the provincial plainness of the furniture. The latter combined a rustic solidity with pleasant Art Nouveau curves. Serrurier-Bovy's philosophy remained unchanged for many years: a room's charm lay in its perimeter – wallpapers *au pochoir*, painted floral ceilings, faience chimney tiles, panelled wainscots, stained-glass windows, and curtains. Favourite themes, which repeated themselves in each medium, were the carrot, umbel, and mimosa. The furniture, however, remained undecorated, no doubt to avoid clashing with its colourful surroundings.

Soon to be published was the firm's sales catalogue. It offered an eclectic range of furnishings including copies of English and American furniture, textiles, carpets, embroideries, silks, oriental ware, and light fixtures. Serrurier-Bovy labelled various suites of furniture after minerals, flowers, and music composers. For example, a bedroom was called 'silex', a dining-room 'cyclamen', and a *salon* 'Wagner'.

Established now as an architect/*ensemblier*, Serrurier-Bovy was exceedingly busy. In 1895, he helped to establish the Salon 'L'Oeuvre Artistique' at the Casino Gréty, in Liège, displaying his furniture alongside the works of Emile Berchmans, Auguste Donnay, Sylvain Dupuis, and Armand Rassenfosse.

In 1896, he showed a bookcase at the Arts and Crafts exhibition in London and then made his début in Paris at the Société Nationale des Beaux-Arts, displaying a library which a critic found 'fresh, innovative, and very practical'. Later that year, he designed a private chapel for the Belgian Minister Braun's house on the rue de Prince Royal in Brussels.

Serrurier-Bovy's preferred furniture wood was oak, especially a Hungarian species. He also used mahogany, padouck, elm, limewood and, at the end of his career, poplar. Except for a varnished finish, he left the surface undecorated, never resorting to paint or marquetry. The only decorative fillip was provided by brightly enamelled panels on the *repoussé* brass and pewter key plates and handles.

Serrurier was commissioned to design the Salle des Importations at the 1897 Exposition Coloniale at Tervuren. His choice of wood for the building's architectural panelling and vitrines was, most appropriately, Congolese Limba. In 1897 and 1898, he exhibited at the Hôtel Chatham in the rue de Ponthieu, Paris, in preference to the Salons. He was busy again in 1899: exhibitions of a mahogany bedroom at the Société d'Art Moderne in Bordeaux and a dining-room at the Société Nationale in Paris crowned a year in which he became internationally known and celebrated for the simplicity and quiet elegance of his designs.

At the Exposition Universelle, Serrurier-Bovy collaborated with René Dulong on the Pavillon Bleu, a first-class restaurant situated at the foot of the Eiffel Tower. The restaurant received considerable publicity in *Le Figaro* . . . for its food!

Interspersed with the expositions were several important architectural commissions which included furniture: a château for M. Verstraete at La Chapelle en Serval; the Cheyrelle Château for M. Jean Felgères at Dienne in Cantal; a studio for the violin virtuoso Eugène Ysaye in Liège; a private chapel for the Abbey Thiéry in Louvain; and the villa 'L'Aube' for himself in Cointe.

By 1902, Serrurier-Bovy had established three retail outlets: his atelier at 39 rue Henricourt, Liège; a gallery at 21 rue de la Blanchisserie, Brussels; and another at 54 rue de Tocqueville, Paris. Four years later he added a fourth in The Hague.

The critics were invariably complimentary to Serrurier-Bovy – it is difficult, in fact, to find even a mildly negative comment on his furniture. Van de Velde, a colleague, was motivated to write a long article in 1902 in *Innendekoration* which included 24 pages of illustrations of Serrurier-Bovy's furniture. Today, however, his pieces often appear rudimentary outside of their original settings. The English Arts and Crafts influence can be too obvious, downplaying Serrurier-Bovy's important contribution to the Art Nouveau movement.

Between 1904 and 1906, he designed several stands for an automobile exposition, including those for Hotchkiss and Jenatzy. In 1910, the furniture-manufacturing atelier closed, and Serrurier-Bovy turned his full attention once more to architecture.

Henry van de Velde
Spokesman, proselytizer, theoretician, and teacher, van de Velde came to the applied arts as an accomplished Impressionist and Pointillist painter. His

decision to forgo his chosen métier was made on viewing a pile of Vincent van Gogh's canvases in his brother's home in Bussum. To van de Velde's ambitious mind, the perfection to which Van Gogh had brought the art of Impressionist painting left nothing for him to achieve. Van de Velde turned promptly to other media, channelling his prodigious energies and talents into book-covers and illustrations, monograms, lecture programmes, wood engravings, silver-ware, glassware, jewelry, and furniture. Soon this restless diversity led him to his own brand of self-taught architecture, the only medium in which he was never quite finally at ease.

Dismayed by the eclecticism of nineteenth-century interiors, he wrote, in his *Formule d'une Esthétique Moderne*, of 'the insane follies which the furniture-makers of past centuries had piled up in bedrooms and drawing-rooms . . . processions of fauns, menacing apocalyptic beasts, benevolently hilarious cupids (bawdy in some cases and complaisantly anxious to please in others), and swollen-checked satyrs in charge of the winds.' To remedy this, he placed emphasis on the interplay of curved lines and empty spaces. Early furniture essays, such as those for his own villa, Bloemenwerf, in Uccle, had a medieval logic and solidity, despite their flowing lines.

A selection of van de Velde's early furniture was illustrated in an exhaustive article in the first issue of *L'Art Décoratif*, 1898. Chairs upholstered in tapestry to his own designs, a stained-glass firescreen, a toiletry table, bookcase, minister's desk, divan with William Morris chintz fabric, and a selection of pieces for Samuel Bing, show a restrained Art Nouveau influence, especially in the feet of his chairs, where an occasional whiplash or volute anticipated his later, more mature 1900 style. The ash bedroom which he showed at the 1898 Art and Crafts exhibition in The Hague illustrates his dependence on colourful wall decoration – painted or stencilled panels, friezes and hangings – to provide an airy and light ambience for his interiors.

Van de Velde appears to have had no preference for a special wood; his furniture, made both at his own atelier in Brussels and by H. Scheidemantel in Weimar, was offered in numerous species, including oak, walnut, teak, padouck, mahogany, beech, cherry and macassar ebony.

Unlike Horta, who designed furniture exclusively for his own buildings, van de Velde undertook outside commissions, for both Meier-Graefe and Bing in Paris and, later, for customers throughout Germany. At the same time that he designed the furnishings for his own buildings (for example, the Esche house in Chemnitz, the Leuring house in Scheveningen, the Folkwang Museum in Hagen, and the Haby barber shop and Havana Co. cigar store in Berlin) there were numerous independent furniture commissions for clients such as Loffler in Berlin, the Osthaus family in Hagen, the Nietzsche Archives, and a Herr

Scheide in Wetter-an-der-Ruhe. Desks, cabinets, bookcases and, most particularly, chairs were produced for many years. Later pieces, often finished in white paint, have stark, rectilinear pre-Bauhaus forms and undisguised screws and joints.

Other important furniture customers included the Keller and Reine art gallery in Berlin and two very private Brussels clients, Mme *S* and Le Baron de *B*, a selection of whose furniture was illustrated in *Innendekoration* in 1898.

Van de Velde's most successful piece of furniture was the large oak desk, conceived in 1896, which he showed at the Munich Secession the following year. Three variations were produced by 1900; the first for Loffler in Berlin, another for Meier-Graefe's office at La Maison Moderne. The four models are now in museums: the Germanisches Museum, Nuremberg; the Nordenfjeldske Kunstindustrimuseum, Trondheim; the Österreichisches Museum, Vienna; and the Hessisches Landesmuseum, Darmstadt.

Unlike that of most of his contemporaries, van de Velde's furniture is almost always stamped with the firm's monogram.

Scotland and England

Forged predominantly by Mackintosh's architectural genius, the Glasgow movement was a team effort that coincided with the public's desire for change within the decorative arts. By sheer chance, talent, commercial motivation and changing taste came together simultaneously to generate a distinctive art movement which eclipsed everything in the United Kingdom to its south. In furniture design, as in most else, it was Mackintosh who predominated. There were others, however, whose creativity must be mentioned.

On a commercial level, the Glasgow firm of Wylie and Lochhead manufactured a wide range of furniture for the middle class, often at aristocratic prices! Today identifiable as midway in style between Art Nouveau and Arts and Crafts – drawing restrained inspiration from both – the firm's design department was largely in the hands of Ernest Archibald Taylor (1874–1951), George Logan and John Ednie.

Taylor trained as a draughtsman in a Clyde shipyard before entering the Glasgow School of Art in the late 1890s. Clearly inspired by the *esprit de corps* of the Glasgow decorative arts community, he adopted several characteristic motifs into his furniture design: the stylized Scottish rose for stained-glass panels and the split heart for the angles on cabinets. His display at the 1902 Turin exhibition included stained-glass panels, two cabinets, a screen and table. A year earlier, his drawing-room for the Wylie and Lochhead pavilion at the Glasgow exhibition showed the dual Edwardian and Glasgow influence on his style. The square frames on his furniture incorporate charming Art Nouveau motifs, themes which continued to the key plates on his doors: for example, those for the dining-room in Lord Weir's house in Pollokshields, a 1901 commission. Two years later, a mahogany desk illustrated in a Wylie and Lochhead catalogue showed Taylor's effective use of the rosebud as decoration.

John Ednie was educated at the Edinburgh School of Art, moving to Glasgow, according to *The Studio*, 'early in the history of the Modern Renaissance and from the beginning was strongly identified with it'. Ednie became a foremost Wylie and Lochhead interior designer, whose work was shown alongside that of Taylor and Logan; often leading to subsequent problems of attribution.

George Logan designed a wide range of items, from metalwork and furniture for Wylie and Lochhead, to ceramics for various Staffordshire potteries. His chairs and cabinets, shown in two rooms of the Glasgow exhibition which *The Studio* illustrated in 1901, were far less inspired than those of his colleagues: sturdy provincial frames belie the proximity of the Glasgow School.

Art Nouveau provided a short chapter in the history of Wylie and Lochhead, which celebrated its 100th anniversary in 1929. The firm's undated catalogues at the turn of the century catered to the Glasgow style; a few years later fashions had changed and the range was dropped. Other Glasgow furniture retailers, such as A. Gardner and Francis Smith, offered a comparable, but less successful, selection of furnishings.

Herbert MacNair was articled in 1888 to Honeyman and Keppie and, as part of his training, attended evening classes at the Glasgow School of Art, where he met Mackintosh, a fellow student. In 1889, Mackintosh joined the firm and for the next six years shared an office with MacNair, no doubt a sufficiently daunting experience to contribute to his decision to leave Glasgow in 1898, by which time Mackintosh had already put his stamp of genius on contemporary architecture.

Notwithstanding, MacNair's few known furniture designs show his pioneership in the Glasgow 'Four'. An oak cabinet, signed and dated in 1895, has a radical form in which MacNair incorporated a favourite motif – a stylized swooping bird in inlaid metal. A table, designed at roughly the same time and now in the library at Hill House, Helensburgh, incorporated three frieze drawers above a carved H-shaped stretcher. At the Turin exhibition, he displayed a writing room which included a charming settee with upholstery embroidered by his wife, and a table veneered in ebony and canarywood. A revolving bookcase, likewise illustrated in *The Studio*, contained a jewelled and leaded-glass gallery. The precision of the furniture, and its placement within the room, made it at first glance indistinguishable from the neighbouring rooms by Mackintosh.

Another to leave Glasgow in 1898, probably for the same reasons as MacNair, was George Walton. Invited by Miss Cranston in 1888 to decorate a smoking room in her tea-room at 114 Argyle Street, Walton forsook his career as a bank clerk to participate in the aesthetic movement. By 1896 his reputation was such that Miss Cranston commissioned him to decorate her expanded new tea-rooms on Buchanan Street. Unfortunately for him, his furnishings were upstaged by the murals and hatracks of his young assistant, Mackintosh. By the following year, their roles were reversed; Mackintosh designed the furniture and Walton the walls and ceilings. Walton clearly felt overshadowed, and left for London the following year. Walton's furniture for Miss Cranston included an armchair with a pierced heart splat, a design later adapted by the Germans, Richard Riemerschmid and Alfred Althaus. A diverse draughtsman whose talents extended to Cluthra glass designs for James Couper and James Powell, Walton later provided a range of carpets and furniture for Liberty in London and the Kodak chain of European stores. The earlier Art Nouveau-inspired designs were gradually replaced by a more formal Aesthetic Movement look.

By 1908, the Glasgow School was dead. Tastes changed rapidly, leaving the movement's protagonists totally unprepared for the loss of commissions and celebrity, a calamity faced by large drinking bouts in Mackintosh's home on Southpark Avenue.

In England, William Morris's apostles did not pursue the natural evolution of his teachings into twentieth-century modernism, as did the Glasgow School and Vienna. English furniture-makers at the turn of the century clung to quasi-eighteenth-century forms enhanced with the newly fashionable Arts and Crafts motifs. None of the London artist/designers who became prominent in other areas of Art Nouveau design – in particular, Ashbee and Voysey – took their furniture designs beyond a sturdy Burges- or Morris-like form; not appreciably different, in fact, from the pieces manufactured by the Guild of Handicraft and the Art Worker's Guild in the 1890s. The earlier chair and cabinet by Mackmurdo, which in its free forms and fretwork plant motifs clearly anticipated an English participation in the Art Nouveau movement, found no later adherents. Even Baillie Scott's interiors in 1898 for the Duke of Hesse's artist colony in Darmstadt must have appeared strangely traditional in form alongside the works of the German participants such as Olbrich and Behrens.

Another accomplished English furniture designer was Ernest Gimson, who in 1894 established a workshop with Sidney and Ernest Barnsley in Pinbury Park, near Cirencester. The severity of his style anticipated the 1920s, however, rather than echoing the prevailing mood of the Belle Epoque.

Charles Rennie Mackintosh

Every aspect of Mackintosh's production – architecture, furniture and paintings – has been analysed in numerous volumes by, *inter alios*, Thomas Howarth, Roger Billcliffe, and Filippo Alison. The work of no other proponent of the Art Nouveau idiom, in fact, has received such repeated and intense scholastic scrutiny – not even Tiffany, Gallé, or Lalique. Mackintosh's Glaswegian training, his marriage to Frances MacDonald, and his leadership of 'The Four' are therefore well known and do not bear repetition here.

Despite his training as an architect, Mackintosh is better known today as a designer of furniture or, more specifically, of chairs. This is ironic, as his furnishings were initially a natural corollary of, and secondary to, his buildings; they were designed to delineate the interior spaces in which his clients would spend most of their time.

Early commissions, such as his designs in 1892–93 for the Glasgow Art Club (while he was articled at Honeyman and Keppie) and his alterations to the entrance hall at Craigie Hall, show an adherence to carved traditional decoration. In 1896, Mackintosh collaborated with George Walton on the interior of Miss Cranston's tea-rooms in Buchanan Street. Although Walton's assistant in the project, it was the young Mackintosh's style and flair that delighted Miss Cranston and which set up his independent commission for her Argyle Street tea-rooms the following year.

In this first major commission to combine architecture and furniture design, bold outlines and box-line shapes identify all the pieces – chairs, settees, benches, card- and domino-tables, and umbrella stands. The architectonic features of Mackintosh's later designs had already matured. Tall, slender back-rests with ladderback splats or pierced oval crests match the soaring linear contours of his buildings. Mackintosh's chosen wood was oak, its rich grain heightened with a clear varnish or, later, as at the Turin Exhibition, painted white.

Mackintosh brought to his furniture the motifs characteristic of all Glasgow School decoration: stylized roses, cabbages, apple pips, trees, and tulips, to list only the most common. Later he introduced attenuated young women onto wallpapers and stencilled upholstery. These were aptly described by the German Hermann Muthesius at the 1902 Turin Exhibition: 'the human figure there seems to be only a creative pretext; by its representation he [the artist] aims at nothing but a soothing lull of lines; it is stretched in length or twisted in all directions according to need, but it always remains exclusively decorative. It is stylized just as English art has stylized the plant . . .' Further decoration was provided by leaded-glass panels set into chair backs, cabinet doors and light fixtures.

Miss Cranston established Mackintosh's reputation internationally, except in England where a sullen silence was interspersed through the years by occasional snipings at each new European acclaim. The Secessionists, in particular, found in Mackintosh's elongated linear style the inspiration for which they had long clamoured. 'The Four's' 1900 exhibition in Vienna showed the host city's natural affinity for the Glasgow movement, an alliance which stepped around and beyond the Art Nouveau movement to lay the foundations for Gropius and the Cubist movement. Richard Muther, in his review of the Glasgow exhibit in Vienna, wrote, 'you will be aware of a great degree of unity of tone. You stand perhaps in the room of Mr and Mrs Mackintosh, you see thin, tall candles, chairs and cupboards thrust upwards in pure verticals, pictures with slender elliptical figures whose outlines are governed by the linear play of a unifying thread.' In Turin two years later, 'The Four' reached their high point; the panegyrics of the judges and international critics put the final stamp of acceptability on their work.

Private commissions accelerated after 1897. Included were the Ingram Street tea-rooms and Main Street flat in 1900; Westel, in Queen's Place, in 1901; the Wärndorfer Musik Salon, Vienna, and the Hill House, Helensburgh, in 1902;

Hous' Hill in 1903; and the Willow Tearooms in 1904. Roger Billcliffe, in his *Charles Rennie Mackintosh: the Complete Furniture, Furniture Drawings and Interior Designs*, estimates that Mackintosh designed well over 400 pieces, mainly between 1897 and 1905 and 1916 and 1918. Most of these included very detailed interiors in which every element of decoration – from the chairs to the cutlery and cruet sets – were created with the same intricacy and care.

Criticism must be voiced of the workmanship of Mackintosh's furniture. The local artisans and joiners, such as Francis Smith, who were commissioned to execute his designs, were totally inexperienced and unqualified to produce premier cabinetwork. It is a curious inconsistency that Mackintosh, who was so precise in his draughtsmanship, should have overlooked, or simply forsaken, the finished item. His furniture was frequently rough-hewn and badly assembled; eighty years later it is often structurally unsound, coming apart under the slightest pressure or weight.

Spain and Italy

The decorative arts suffered a creative vacuum in the Mediterranean countries at the turn of the century; following the shoreline from Gibraltar to Palermo, one finds that only in Barcelona was there a concerted movement, but even there it was half-hearted and largely fruitless. The genius of Spain's contemporary painters – Picasso, Gris, Dali and Miró – was absent within the applied arts. The Spanish version of Art Nouveau, *El Modernisme*, was almost entirely limited to the buildings of a small group of Catalan architects. The architecture of Luis Doménech y Montaner (1850–1923), Rafael Massó, Henrique Sagnier, José Puig y Cadafalch, and others, shows a sympathy for German Secessionists such as Behrens and Loos. It was Doménech, incidentally, who tried to pioneer a Spanish revival in the decorative arts inspired by the English Arts and Crafts movement, the fruits of which are today virtually invisible. Drawing also on a series of publications written in the 1870s by Spanish critics such as Senpere y Miquel and Miquel y Badía, Doménech spoke out frequently on the need for a renaissance.

Apart from Gaudí, three other designers turned their energies to Art Nouveau furniture: Alejo Clapes Puig, Gaspar Homar, and Juan Busquets.

The furniture designs of *Antoni Gaudí*, Catalonia's great turn-of-the-century architect, were limited to the interiors of his buildings. His brilliant architectural eccentricity is now internationally known and appreciated; the few pieces of his furniture that reach the open market today reflect, in their frenzied prices, the esteem in which Gaudí's work at large is held. Certainly nobody else's rough-hewn oak double pew would generate such spirited bidding at auction. As with Mackintosh, it is not, happily, the cabinetry which is at issue, rather the creative stamp of a brilliant individualist.

Gaudí was born in Rens in the province of Tarragona. In 1878, on completing his degree in architecture, he met his future patron, Eusebio Güell y Bacigalupi. In the same year came his first furniture design, that for his own desk. A curious baroque structure with curved cupboards and twin pedestal drawers raised on spindly feet, it anticipated his future break with convention. Next came the commission for a funerary chapel for the first Marquis of Comillas, in Comillas, near Santander, for which Gaudí designed a neo-classical chair and stool. A corner cabinet for the Casa Vicens was likewise traditional, having a heavily carved and hinged Renaissance look. Later came a design for a monstrance and a showcase for the glovemaker Esteban Camella's exhibit at the 1879 Exposition Universelle.

Soon Gaudí's architectural flare had assured him an abundance of commissions. In 1885 he began his design for Güell's house at No 3/5, the Calle Conda de Asalto, Barcelona. The furnishings included an odd kidney-shaped *chaise longue* with tufted upholstery inspired by the cross-section of a chambered nautilus shell, and a dressing table, both of which defy easy categorization.

A chair with padded armrests terminating in carved dragons showed that he clung for some time to conventional concepts of furniture design; it was only in 1898, when he began work on the Casa Calvet, that a complete break with tradition became evident. The oak chairs and benches have shield-shaped backs pierced with trefoil leaf motifs which suggest identification with his Art Nouveau cohorts to the North. There is a cavalier Guimard defiance to their free forms and a Mackintosh disregard for their rudimentary finish. Gaudí's *prie-dieux* for the chapel of the Colona Güell, begun in the same year, incorporated the same combination of visionary design and rigorous woodwork. In 1906 came his designs for the Casa Battló. The chairs, designed as double- and seven-seated units, were angled variations on the Casa Calvet models.

Throughout his career, Gaudí continued to mix revolutionary Art Nouveau designs with tradition. The church of the Sagrada Familia was furnished with stiffly traditional eighteen-legged pews and a wooden pulpit; the seats in the Parque Güell and Santa Coloma de Cervelo followed a broad serpentine sweep in keeping with the 1900 movement.

Alejo Clapés Puig (1850–1920) was born in San Ginés de Vilasar, near Barcelona. Apprenticed in the studio of the artist Hernandez, Clapés later enrolled in the Barcelona School of Arts where he was instructed by Claudio Lorenzale. Sojourns in Paris and Rome preceded his return to Barcelona where he established himself as a portrait- and religious painter. Retained by Gaudí to help in the decorations of the Palacio Güell, Clapés' contribution included a mural and several decorative panels. Occasional furniture commissions followed. Clearly influenced by what he had seen at the Palacio Güell, Clapés appears to have attempted to go even beyond Gaudí: the suite of *salon* furniture which he designed for the Ibarz house in Barcelona (now in the Museo Gaudí), including a vitrine, chairs, sofa, and *porte-manteau*, is as outrageously Art Nouveau as one can imagine, in its carved drapes and sweeping organic legs exceeding anything that Paris or Nancy dared to conceive.

Juan Busquets Jane (1874–1949) received his initial training as a cabinetmaker and decorator at the Barcelona School of Arts and then in his father's furniture studio. Established on his own in 1895, one of his first commissions was for the living-room for A. Manuel Felip. The next year Busquets won a scholarship to the Spanish School of Fine Arts, receiving an honorary mention in the School's competition that year. By 1898 he had adopted fully the Art Nouveau style, showing several pieces at the Fourth General Exposition of Beaux-Arts in Barcelona. After 1900 his florid style softened somewhat; a Viennese influence is more readily recognizable. Busquets continued to produce Art Nouveau-inspired furniture for many years: as late as 1911 an *armoire*, with enamel inlay, presented at the Sixth International Exposition of Art in Barcelona, contained the serpentine contours so characteristic of his earlier work. The piece is now in the Barcelona Museum of Art.

Like Busquets, *Gaspar Homar Mezquida* (1870–1953) was a cabinetmaker and decorator, gaining his experience in the studio of the furniture-maker, Francisco Vidal. Producing Gothic-style pieces, he established himself in the Rambla de Cataluña in 1893. Within four years, however, when he moved to Canuda Street, his work showed a strong Art Nouveau influence; not only the furniture, but ceilings, walls, stained-glass panels, lamps, and carpets; i.e., all elements of design. A characteristic of his furniture was the use of marquetry panels — most often in beds, *armoires*, and cabinets – in which flower-bedecked young ladies frolic in summer landscapes, their faces and hands finely carved in low relief. Homar drew on the talents of draughtsmen and artisans in José Pey for the designs and execution of these pieces. Numerous commissions followed. Interiors for the Burés and Navás houses in 1901; the Lleó Morera house by Luis Doménech y Montaner in 1904; a bedroom and living-room for the Oliva house; the Par de Mesa house; furnishings for the Marquis of Marianao; the Arumi house, and many more. At the same time he exhibited at the annual expositions: in 1904 in London and Barcelona; in 1908 in Zaragoza and Venice; in 1909 in Paris.

Homar continued to produce modern furniture until 1918, when he abruptly switched from his own designs to the commercial reproduction of Renaissance-style models.

Italian Art Nouveau furniture, like that in Spain, was dominated by a single man, Carlo Bugatti, one whose monolithic contribution is discussed below. Beyond Bugatti, the *style nouille*, as the French critics were quick to label the sinuous Italian version of Art Nouveau, was limited largely to architects such as Pietro Fenoglio, Alfredo Premoli, and Raimondo d'Aronco. Only after World War II did Italy have a major impact on interior design, most particularly in lighting fixtures and furniture.

The Italian pavilions at the 1900 Exposition Universelle and in Turin two years later received universal censure. A critic in *The Studio* wrote of the Turin edifice that 'the whole effect of it was that of a huge bazaar, rather than an exhibition of artistic work'. Nobody else tried to match Bugatti's idiosyncratic flare. Eugenio Quarti (1867–1931), a fellow Milanese and close friend, adopted a restrained Art Nouveau style of furniture design based on the Parisian volute. Quarti produced a wide range of furniture styles, dropping the Art Nouveau models after 1906 when the style's excesses had led to its abrupt eclipse. At the 1906 Milan exhibition, his pieces were more restrained than earlier, leaning in their influence away from Paris towards Vienna. Another Art Nouveau cabinetmaker, Carlo Zen (1851–1918), displayed at most major exhibitions. The father of Pietro Zen, a noted designer whose rectilinear style was a direct antithesis of his father's, Carlo embraced the Art Nouveau doctrine at its most florid and curvaceous: a settee designed in 1902 has a tapestried back-rest beneath an elaborately scrolled crest-rail into which was fitted a mirror, reminiscent of the *chaise longue* by Tony Selmersheim at the Paris Salon the previous year. Other pieces incorporated floral marquetry on lightly structured frames.

Bugatti

Described by the critic Maxime LeRoy in 1903 as 'an isolated genius whose flare for the bizarre defies classification', Bugatti carried the Art Nouveau banner in Italy virtually single-handedly. His interpretation of the new art was utterly unique, drawing on a marvellous hotchpotch of Hispano-Moresque architectural influences painted with Japanese bamboo shoots and other exoticism.

Pseudo-Arabic minarets, dentils, and spindled galleries silhouette the outlines of furniture designed on the circle and its parts – the arc and chord. The wooden frame was covered in chamois leather within *repoussé* metal mounts or veneered in pewter and brass with insect-like motifs and Middle Eastern calligraphy. Tassels, either singly or in fringes, added to the theatrical effect.

The critics were variously perplexed, excited and angered. Bugatti's exhibit at the 1888 Italian Exposition at Earl's Court in London was found by the critic for *The Queen, the Lady's Newspaper* to be quaint and 'in Mauresque style'. The nine accompanying line drawings show that the architectural style for which his furniture is now best known had already matured: chairs with gong-shaped splats suspended by twisted silk cords and wall *étagères* with ebonized parapet supports and arched friezes. Not everybody was favourably impressed, however. The price of individualism is that it *is* different. Bugatti's style was to many ponderous, devoid of the airiness and fluidity that the new art was meant to espouse. One critic, on viewing the bedroom which Lord Battersea commissioned for his London home, *c.* 1900, found the only merit of the visit to be that it saved him the cost of a train ride to Grenada to see the Alhambra!

Post-1900 saw a distinct and final evolution in Bugatti's style. His furniture at the Turin Exhibition was sharply different from his earlier *oeuvres*. Vellum, previously limited to the large undecorated expanses on his furniture, such as chair seats and panelling on screens and cupboards, now predominated. Chairs were completely covered, their seams neatly stitched and concealed.

Bugatti's 'Snail' room in Turin, one of four complete *ensembles* displayed, emphasized the striking modernity of his new furniture; the unbroken sweep from their pierced circular back-rests down, and through, their short feet to the flat circular seat, resembled an upended snail. The pale beige vellum covering appears, at first glance, to be plastic, giving the impression that the chairs were made of injection-moulded plastic, a commercial reality that came to maturity fifty years later. The walls in the Snail room were designed as a series of large circular panels resembling the mollusk's back, beneath which ran a long serpentine couch. An adjoining room was equally striking. The bold sweep of the furniture appears unprecedented, although Bugatti retained several of his earlier circular *repoussé* metal mounts as decoration.

Bugatti was born in Milan on 16 February 1856, the son of Giovanni Luigi, a sculptor. His eccentric style presumes a lack of formal artistic instruction, a mis-supposition which Bugatti himself and many later *aficionados* tried to re-inforce. He had, however, attended Milan's Brera School of Fine Arts in the late 1870s before a sojourn at the Ecole des Beaux-Arts in Paris. Early ambitions in architecture were put aside for a career in cabinetmaking.

In 1905 Bugatti ceased to manufacture furniture, selling the reproduction rights to the Milan firm of De Vecchi. The restless energy apparent in his furniture now began to manifest itself in other media, most particularly silver, in which he collaborated successfully with the firm of A. A. Hebrard after moving to Paris in 1904.

Carlo died in Molshein in 1940, eight years after the tragic death of his daughter and five years after that of his wife, Therese. His artistic genius passed to his two surviving children, Ettore and Rembrandt, the former the creator of *de luxe* motor cars and the latter of animalier bronzes. Few families could boast such genetic prodigy within two short generations.

Germany and Austria

In the late 1800s, Germany was the first country squarely to face the consequences of the machine and its imminent offspring, mass-production furniture. Awareness of the machine's impact on design and, more particularly, of its decorative limitations – i.e., its inability to duplicate the sculpted and veneered decoration of a skilled wood-carver and marqueteur – turned many designers away from the prevailing floral ornateness of French and Belgian furniture. The search was for a viable alternative: design in which function, rather than superficial decoration, would be the criterion of beauty.

The pages of the reviews *Innendekoration* and *Kunst und Kunsthandwerk* illustrate amply that German designers did not respond to the Art Nouveau idiom with either the enthusiasm or the spontaneity of their neighbours. In fact, the exception proved the rule: in furniture, the few truly *Jugendstil* pieces by Endell, Behrens, and Pankok, for example, appear overly exuberant, if not undisciplined, when juxtaposed with those of their Munich Secession colleagues. The critic for *The Studio* wrote, in 1901, that 'there is more sobriety, more judgement in the decoration of the Secessionist galleries than in French furniture.' 'Judgement' was perhaps an inappropriate word at a time when the critics in *Pan* and *Jugend* were demanding that German furniture designers slough off traditionalism – especially the prevailing infatuation with eighteenth-century English and Biedermeier styles – and collaborate in Europe's pursuit of a new beginning. By 1907, however, when the Munich Werkbund was formed, Art Nouveau's international impetus was spent. Germany's earlier restraint was seen, in retrospect, as an alignment with the Wiener Werkstätte.

Notwithstanding the general absence of an Art Nouveau influence, several pieces of furniture by German designers bear mention. In Bavaria, *Richard Riemerschmid* designed a range of furniture – mainly chairs – in mahogany, ash, and poplar. Quiet and rational shapes borrow an occasional volute or scroll from the Art Nouveau vernacular. Riemerschmid's work was manufactured by at least four cabinet shops: the Vereinigte Werkstätte für Kunst im Handwerk (Munich); Kohlbecher und Sohn (Munich); the Deutsche Werkstätte für Handwerkskunst (Dresden-Hellerau); and Theodor Reimann (Dresden). Commissions for private clients were often shown at the yearly Salons; for example, chairs at both the Crystal Palace in Munich and the Deutsche Kunstausstellung in Dresden. Other commissions – for example, a grand piano and lady's desk – were illustrated in *L'Art Décoratif* in 1899.

Also in Munich, *Bernhard Pankok* (1872–1943) designed various pieces with a lightly pronounced Art Nouveau flavour; drawing-room and bedroom furniture in Hungarian ash and oak were executed for him by the Vereinigte Werkstätte für Kunst im Handwerk. His *salon* suite for Dr Krug of Freiburg, in 1902, was widely acclaimed in *Innendekoration*.

Hermann Obrist (1863–1927) was another Munich designer to have his furniture manufactured by the Vereinigte Werkstätte.

Pankok's frequent collaborator, *Bruno Paul* (1874–1968), likewise had his furniture made by the Vereinigte Werkstätte für Kunst im Handwerk, preferring oak, mahogany and walnut for his commissions. One of these – a suite of seat furniture for the Governor of the Beirut province in the Lebanon – was exhibited in 1902 and 1904 at both the Turin and St Louis Expositions. In 1905, a further selection of lightly decorated chairs was shown at the exhibition of the Vereinigung für Angewandte Kunst in Munich.

Peter Behrens (1868–1940), the prominent professor of architecture who included among his students the august threesome of Gropius, van der Rohe, and Le Corbusier, designed a select number of pieces of furniture, including those for his house in the Mathildenhöhe colony, Darmstadt, into which he moved in 1899. At the 1902 Turin exposition, he designed the vestibule for the German pavilion. The pair of winged female figures which flanked the central fountain were themselves flanked by furniture which, in its restrained organic lines, reiterated Germany's reluctance to embrace fully France's momentary infatuation with the new style.

August Endell (1871–1925) was another to produce a limited amount of Art Nouveau-inspired furniture, both before and after his appointment as Director of the Akademie für Kunst und Kunstgewerbe in Breslau. Open armchairs with sculpted knopped finials and capitals recall Guimard's pieces for the Castel Béranger. Earlier, tables executed in 1899 by the Deutsche Werkstätte für Handwerkskunst in Dresden-Hellerau, were commissioned by the sanatorium at Wyth am Föhr.

Otto Eckmann, another member of the Munich Secession, was commissioned by the Grand Duke Ernst Ludwig von Hessen to submit interior designs for his palace near Darmstadt. Eckmann selected exotic woods for his furniture: American beech, Gabonese elm, and ash. Others were made of steel. Several pieces are now in the Hessisches Landesmuseum. Also in Darmstadt was *Patriz Huber*, whose furniture was executed by Hofmöbelfabrik Glückert. Huber's oak and cherrywood chairs have a stiff Arts and Crafts appearance, despite his claim in an *Innendekoration* advertisement that he was in the vanguard of *Jugendstil*.

In Dresden, *Albin Müller* showed his furniture at the Kunstgewerbeausstellung. Rectangular structures are enhanced with floral and scrolled brass key plates and door hinges. Also in Dresden were Otto Fischer, Johann Cissarz,

Professor Karl Gross, and E. Schaudt. In Düsseldorf, Professor G. Oeder designed a range of Art Nouveau furniture, while in Leipzig F. A. Schütz included a similar range of furniture in his sales catalogues.

As for Austria, the founding of the breakaway Secession in March 1897 marked the beginning of a new artistic era. Among the group's protagonists were several young men already prominent in their respective fields – Gustav Klimt, Josef Olbrich, and Josef Hoffmann – whose aim was to exhibit their own work, and that of foreign avant-gardists, free from the restraints of the reactionary Artists' House organization.

The early Secessionist style took as its inspiration Mackintosh's architectural and furniture designs, which were further entrenched by the Glasgow Four's participation in the Vienna Secession's eighth exhibition in 1900. Whereas Mackintosh's elongated linear style was highly popular, the Secessionists soon rejected his heavy decorative imagery – the symbolist rose and attenuated virginal maidens – in favour of their own stark and achromatic forms of decoration.

In 1903, with the backing of a young banker, Fritz Wärndorfer, Hoffmann and Moser founded the Wiener Werkstätte-Produktiv-Gemeinschaft von Kunsthandwerken, an association whose aim was to unite masters and artisans in the pursuit of 'an entire art environment'.

In the early years, all designs were by the two artistic directors. Within a short time, however, other designers and architects were drawn in, amongst them Klimt, Adolf Loos, Czeschka, Wagner, and Löffler. The number of masters quickly swelled to 37, that of employees to 100.

The Wiener Werkstätte's early furniture was relatively simple. Hoffmann's designs, in particular, showed either a Mackintosh or English Arts and Crafts influence. By 1908, however, exotic woods and rich veneers combined with sharper angularity to anticipate the magnificence of French Art Deco furniture.

A major commission was soon forthcoming: the Brussels house of a rich bourgeois, Adolphe Stoclet. Given total freedom, the Wiener Werkstätte chose a sumptuous array of glass, marble and woods to carry the banner of Viennese modernism into the heart of Art Nouveau's founding city. No project in Austria ever attained the same thoroughness or opulence. Throughout were brilliant solutions to modern design problems, from bathtubs to bookbindings. The house's furniture, designed by Hoffmann and Moser, picked up the stark contours of the building's façade.

Josef Hoffmann (1870–1956) was born in Pirnitz, Moravia, on 15 December 1870. Having studied at the Crafts School in Brno, he went to Vienna in 1892 to enroll in the School of Applied Arts. In 1896, he entered the Vienna School of Art and the following year became a full professor of architecture.

Hoffmann's genius and energies pervaded the artistic events of turn-of-the-century Vienna. Not only was he a co-founder of both the Secession and the Wiener Werkstätte, but he led by example: designs for book-covers, jewelry, silverware, plant stands, lamps, houses and hippodromes poured off his sketch pad at breakneck speed, all imbued with his total comprehension of the new fashions in art and architecture.

His 1901 essay 'Simple Furniture' illustrated a cross-section of his early models. Mackintosh's influence is ever-present. Soon, however, Hoffmann's functionalism superseded the Scot's aesthetics. As A. S. Levetus wrote in 1906 of Hoffmann's furniture, 'utility is the first condition, but there is no reason why the simplest articles should not be beautiful. The value does not lie only in the material, but in the right thought and treatment of the material, and its power to convey that thought to the minds of others, to convince them. This is no easy task.'

Soon Hoffmann and his pupils were producing clean, cubic, twentieth-century objects, especially in glass, ceramics, and metal. Ancillary furnishings – umbrella-stands, *jardinières*, centrepieces, flower pots – incorporated his pierced latticework (*quadratisch*) and black-and-white checkerboard (*Gitterwerk*) decorative themes.

Hoffmann's furniture designs were prolific, many manufactured in elm or beech bentwood by Kohn, Thonet, Anton Pospischil and, of course, the Wiener Werkstätte.

Two furniture commissions merit special mention. The first was Hoffmann's chair designs for the Purkersdorf sanitorium, near Vienna, in 1904–05. The variety of elegant side- and dining-chairs with pierced oval back-rests and splats are today immediately identifiable as Hoffmann masterpieces.

Later, in 1907, came his commission for the *Kabarett Fledermaus*, the watering hole of fashionable Vienna. Hoffmann's designs for the interior were dazzlingly neat and uncluttered: utilitarian tables and chairs with ball joints were painted in spartan black and white. Opening with Oskar Kokoschka's *The Spotted Egg*, the playhouse was soon frequented more by design students than theatre buffs. The chairs, now often overpainted, are classics of twentieth-century design.

Otto Wagner (1841–1918) gave his name to an entire generation of early modern Viennese designers – *die Wagnerschule*. Architect, city planner and designer, Wagner taught at the Vienna School of Art from 1894 to 1912, bringing his influence to bear on Richard Neutra, Rudolph Schindler, and many others.

Wagner's philosophy was based on a functionalist aesthetic: his designs were basically cubic, inspired by utility and common sense. As a member of the

Secession from 1899 to 1905, he designed several pieces of furniture in beech-wood manufactured by both Thonet and Kohn. The stiff rectilinear forms showed their architectural derivation.

Architect and author *Adolf Loos* (1870–1923) was born in Moravia, receiving his diploma from the Institute of Technology in Dresden. Like Hoffmann, Loos is now recognized as a pioneer of modern architecture. Although he raged continually against all forms of ornamentation, the chairs which he designed show a delicate sweep which can be interpreted as a concession to the prevailing taste. His interior for the Café Museum in 1899, which became the prototype for avant-garde Viennese cubism, included chairs and tables in birch and walnut.

A large proportion of the bentwood furniture designed in Vienna at the turn of the century was made either by Thonet Brothers or Jacob and Josef Kohn. Competition was fierce; only in 1923, when the two merged with sixteen other bentwood manufacturers to become the Thonet-Mundus Company, was the arch-rivalry resolved. Designers such as Hoffmann and Moser appear to have switched their patronage at will. No identifiable pattern emerges in the type of furniture commissioned from either firm. In addition, Thonet had its own in-house designers – for example, Ullmann, Siegl, and Holzmeister – to produce its own wide range of furniture. In 1904, over 1200 models were listed in the firm's sales catalogue.

The bentwood technique met perfectly the Secessionists' needs for modern furniture construction. Developed by Michael Thonet in the 1830s and '40s, bentwood was spartan, trim, and unpretentious; its malleability adapting to the most gentle or complex scrolled or whiplash back-rest or stretcher. Many Secessionists considered it fundamental to sound design, among them Gustav Siegl, Josef Urban, Marcel Kammerer, Fritz Nagl, and Anton Lorenz.

Closely aligned to Hoffmann, *Koloman Moser* (1868–1918) was an artist turned designer. Between 1886 and 1895, he attended first the Viennese Academy and then the School of Arts and Crafts. In 1897, he was a co-founder of the Secession Group, returning to the School of Arts and Crafts in 1899 as a professor. Moser designed a wide range of furnishings – rugs, vases, tableware, light fixtures and stained-glass windows. His furniture, mostly executed by Kohn, included a dining-room suite in mahogany and sycamore inlaid with brass, and beechwood chairs painted white and with aluminium shoes. Smaller items, such as his stepped square metal plant-stands and candlesticks, are often indistinguishable from those of Hoffmann.

Born in Troppau in Silesia, *Josef M. Olbrich* (1867–1908) studied under both K. V. Hagenauer and Otto Wagner before becoming a co-founder of the Secession Group. Two years later he moved to Darmstadt, where he continued his work as architect, designer, and painter. The retrospective exhibition of his work at the Hessisches Landesmuseum in 1967 showed his multifarious talents: light fixtures, furniture, clocks, building exteriors, boat interiors, etc. His furniture for Princess Elisabeth von Hessen's Wolfsgarten Castle on the Rhine has a charming lightness: the yellow pinewood armchairs and sofa have arched back-rests upholstered in cotton with a repeating oval geometric pattern enclosing the letter 'E'. His sketches for a wide selection of mantel and long-case clocks have the same angular crispness; uncluttered contours enhanced with black-and-white checkerboard motifs. Another clock, exhibited at Turin in 1902, incorporated the same architectural influences.

Bibliography

Designers' Bibliographies

Index

Bibliography

Allgemeines Lexikon der bildenden Künstler, Leipzig 1907
Amayo, Mario *Art Nouveau*, London/New York 1966
Art Nouveau: Art and Design at the Turn of The Century,
  The Museum of Modern Art, New York 1959

Barilli, Renato *Art Nouveau*, London 1966
Borsi, Franco *Bruxelles 1900*, Paris 1974
Bossaglia, R. *Le Mobilier Art Nouveau*, Paris 1972
Brosio, Valentino *Le Stile Liberty*, Milan 1967

Cassou, Jean; Langui, Emile; and Pevsner, Nikolaus
  Sources of Modern Art, London 1962
Champigneulle, B. *L'Art Nouveau*, Paris 1972

Dingelstedt, K. *Le Modern Style dans les arts appliqués*,
  Paris 1959
Drexler, Arthur and Daniel, Greta *Introduction to Twentieth
  Century Design from the collection of The Museum of Modern
  Art, New York*, New York 1959

Europa 1900, Brussels 1967 (exhibition catalogue)
Europäischer Jugendstil, Bremen 1965 (exhibition catalogue)
*L'exposition universelle internationale: Rapport du comité
  d'installation*, Paris 1900

Graham, F. Lanier, *Hector Guimard*, New York 1970
  (catalogue of exhibition at The Museum of Modern Art)

Henry van de Velde, Brussels 1970 (exhibition catalogue)
Howarth, Thomas *Charles Rennie Mackintosh and the
  Modern Movement*, London 1952
Hüter, Karl-Heinz *Henry van de Velde*, Berlin 1967

Joseph M. Olbrich, 1867–1908, Das Werk des Architekten,
  Hessisches Landesmuseum, Darmstadt 1967

Mackay, James *Turn-of-the-Century Antiques*, London 1974
Macleod, Robert, *Charles Rennie Mackintosh*, Feltham 1968
Madsen, Stephen Tschudi *Sources of Art Nouveau*, Oslo
  1916

L'oeuvre de Rupert Carabin, 1862–1932, Luxembourg 1974
  (exhibition catalogue)
Pevsner, Nikolaus *Pioneers of Modern Design*, New York
  1949

Revue de l'exposition universelle de 1889, Paris 1889
Rheims, Maurice *L'objet 1900*, Paris 1964

Secession: Europäische Kunst um die Jahrhundertwende,
  Munich 1964 (exhibition catalogue)
Les sources du 20e siècle: les arts en Europe de 1884 à 1914,
  Paris 1960 (exhibition catalogue)

Tierlinck, Herman *Henry van de Velde*, Brussels 1959

Um 1900, Art Nouveau und Jugendstil, Zurich 1952
  (exhibition catalogue)
Um 1900: Die neue Sammlung, Munich 1969 (exhibition
  catalogue)

Victor Horta, son Musée, Brussels n.d.
Vienna Secession, Art Nouveau to 1970, London 1971
  (exhibition catalogue)

Watelet, J. C. *Le Décorateur Liégeois: Gustave Serrurier-Bovy,
  1858–1910*, Cahiers Henry van de Velde, no. 11,
  Brussels 1970
Weber, Wilhelm *Peter Behrens (1868–1940)*, Kaiserslautern
  1966 (exhibition catalogue)
Werke un 1900, Berlin 1966 (exhibition catalogue)

Designers' Bibliographies

ANDRÉ, Emile
La Lorraine Artiste, No. 20, 15 June 1899, pp. 12, 40
                               1902, pp. 177–80
                               1903, p. 82
L'Art Décoratif, Jan.–June 1903, p. 178
Art et Décoration, Jan.–June 1903, p. 132
Bulletin des Sociétés Artistiques de l'Est, No. 12, Dec. 1904,
  p. 221

ANGST, Albert
Art et Décoration, Jan.–June 1897, pp. 78, 80
                   Jan.–June 1899, p. 87
                   Jan.–June 1901, p. 130
                   Jan.–June 1902, pp. 183, 186
Meubles et Décors, Nos. 815/816, June 1966, p. 70
L'Art Décoratif, Jan.–June 1905, pp. 259–60

BELLERY-DESFONTAINES, Henri-Jules-Ferdinand
Art et Décoration, July–Dec. 1897, pp. 56–59
                   July–Dec. 1898, pp. 13–15
                   June–Dec. 1899, p. 46
                   July–Dec. 1900, pp. 146, 148
                   Jan.–June 1904, pp. 12, 14
                   Jan.–June 1907, pp. 162–67
                   July–Dec. 1907, p. 156
L'Art Décoratif, July 1900, p. 145
              July–Dec. 1907, p. 164
Meubles et Décors, Nos. 815/816, June 1966, p. 80

BELVILLE, Eugène
Art et Décoration, Jan.–June 1897, pp. 76, 78
                   July–Dec. 1898, p. 11
                   July–Dec. 1900, p. 145
                   Jan.–July 1902, p. 180
L'Art Décoratif, Jan. 1903, p. 214

BENOUVILLE, Léon
L'Art Décoratif, July–Dec. 1900, p. 68, 70
               July–Dec. 1901, pp. 160, 195
               July–Dec. 1902, p. 167
               Jan.–June 1903, pp. 210–11
Art et Décoration, Jan.–June 1897, p. 105
                   Jan.–June 1901, p. 199
                   July–Dec. 1901, p. 34
                   Jan.–June 1902, p. 180
                   Jan.–June 1903
Revue des Arts Décoratifs, 1901, p. 201
Meubles et Décors, No. 817, August 1966, p. 98

BIGAUX, Louis
L'Art Décoratif, July–Dec. 1902, p. 170
               July–Dec. 1906, p. 207
Art et Décoration, July–Dec. 1897, p. 57
                   Jan.–June 1898, p. 68
                   Jan.–June 1900, p. 105
                   July–Dec. 1900, p. 143
                   Jan.–June 1902, p. 184
                   July–Dec. 1907, p. 201
Art et Industrie (Nancy), 1911, p. 57
Revue des Arts Décoratifs, 1900, p. 76

BOVERIE, Joseph
L'Art Décoratif, April 1902, p. 17
La Revue des Arts Décoratifs, 1902, p. 96
Art et Décoration, July–Dec. 1901, pp. 120, 124

CARABIN, Rupert
L'Art Décoratif, Jan.–June 1901, p. 139
               July–Dec. 1903, p. 65
               Jan.–June 1905, p. 258
Meubles et Décors, No. 809, December 1965, Ills. 12–14
Art et Décoration, Jan.–June 1900, p. 130
Art et Industrie (Nancy) 1909, p. 109
                         1910, pp. 101–04
La Revue d'Art, 1900, pp. 161–68
'L'oeuvre de Rupert Carabin, 1862–1932', Galerie du
  Luxembourg, exhibition catalogue, Paris 1974

CHARPENTIER, Alexandre
The Studio, March 1897, pp. 125–26
            March 1898, pp. 83–84
Art et Décoration, July–Dec. 1898, p. 19
                   Jan.–June 1899, p. 101
                   July–Dec. 1899, p. 46
                   Jan.–June 1900, p. 12, 47–49, 115
                   July–Dec. 1900, pp. 33–41, 18
                   Jan.–June 1901, pp. 134, 139, 196–98
                   Jan.–June 1902, pp. 180–182
                   July–Dec. 1902, pp. 4, 6
Revue des Arts Décoratifs, 1900, p. 260
                          1901, pp. 202–04, 97–103
L'Art Décoratif, May 1901, pp. 52–53
              July–Dec. 1901, pp. 158–61
              July–Dec. 1902, p. 171
              Jan.–June 1904, p. 98
Meubles et Décors, No. 813, April 1966, p. 77–79

COLONNA, Edouard
Art et Décoration, Jan.–June 1899, p. 101
Jan.–June 1900, pp. 114–16
July–Dec. 1900, pp. 35, 43–44, 137, 149
July–Dec. 1901, pp. 33, 118
The Studio, XX, 1900, pp. 166–77
Revue des Arts Décoratifs, 1900, pp. 258–66
L'Art Décoratif, Jan.–June 1900, pp. 92–96
July–Dec. 1900, pp. 174–75

CROIX-MARIE, Paul
L'Art Décoratif, Jan.–June 1901, p. 161
July–Dec. 1904, pp. 94, 98
Jan.–June 1905, p. 264
July–Dec. 1906, p. 207
Art et Décoration, Jan.–June 1904, pp. 88–89

DAMON & COLIN
L'Art Décoratif, Jan.–June 1900, pp. 214–16
July–Dec. 1902, p. 301
Art et Décoration, Jan.–June 1900, p. 117
July–Dec. 1900, pp. 138–42
Meubles et Décors, Nos. 815/816, June 1960, p. 68

DAMPT, Jean-Auguste
Meubles et Décors, No. 810, January 1966, p. 36
L'Art Décoratif, July–Dec. 1899, p. 161
April 1901, pp. 45–46
July–Dec. 1902, p. 172
July–Dec. 1903, p. 62
Art et Décoration, Jan.–June 1897, pp. 72–74
July–Dec. 1898, p. 19
Jan.–June 1899, p. 86
July–Dec. 1899, p. 47
Jan.–June 1900, p. 12, 48
Jan.–June 1901, pp. 129, 140
Jan.–June 1902, p. 186
Jan.–June 1906, p. 116
The Studio, March 1897, p. 121
March 1898, p. 73
Revue des Arts Décoratifs, 1901, pp. 101–02
1903, p. 366

DE FEURE, Georges
Revue des Arts Décoratifs, 1900, pp. 258, 263–67
1901, pp. 206–07
L'Art Décoratif, Jan.–June 1900, pp. 90–97, 217, 218–28
July–Dec. 1900, pp. 174–75
Jan.–June 1901, pp. 23–29, 116–17,
118–19, 124
July–Dec. 1901, pp. 144–48
July–Dec. 1902, p. 172
Art et Décoration, Jan.–June 1900, p. 115
July–Dec. 1900, pp. 35, 146, 148

Jan.–June 1901, pp. 79–84, 198
July–Dec. 1901, pp. 117, 119, 121–24,
156–60
Jan.–June 1902, p. 178
July–Dec. 1908, pp. 115–32
The Studio, XX, 1900, pp. 170–80

FÉREZ
La Lorraine Artiste, 1899, p. 39
1901, p. 295
L'Art Décoratif, Jan.–June, 1905

GAILLARD, Eugène
L'Art Décoratif, Jan.–June 1900, pp. 89, 94
July–Dec. 1901, pp. 124, 170–73
Jan.–June 1902, p. 22
July–Dec. 1902, pp. 166, 172
Jan.–June 1903, pp. 214–16
July–Dec. 1903, p. 239
July–Dec. 1906, pp. 23, 30, 203, 204, 216
Jan.–June 1907, p. 167
Art et Décoration, Jan.–June 1900, p. 112
July–Dec. 1900, pp. 36, 41–45
Jan.–June 1901, pp. 193, 199
July–Dec. 1901, p. 33
Jan.–June 1902, pp. 21–27, 180, 186
Jan.–June 1907, p. 164
July–Dec. 1907, p. 201
July–Dec. 1913, pp. 26, 27
Art et Industrie, Jan. 1911, p. 37
Revue des Arts Décoratifs, 1900, pp. 254–67
1901, pp. 206, 210, 100
The Studio, XX, 1900, pp. 166, 174, 176, 178–79

GALLÉ, Emile
Art et Industrie (Nancy), July 1909, pp. 77–89
1910, p. 79ff
Jan. 1911, p. 115
L'Art Décoratif, July–Dec. 1901, p. 19
July–Dec. 1902, pp. 169, 172
Jan. 1903, pp. 176–77, 180, 212–14
Jan.–June 1905, pp. 97–98, 101–03,
111–12, 126–35, 259–60
Emile Gallé, F.-T. Charpentier, Université de Nancy II,
Nancy, 1978
Emile Gallé, Philippe Garnier, London 1978
Europa 1900, Ostende, exhibition catalogue, No. 49
Art et Décoration, Jan.–June 1898, p. 108, 110, 112
July–Dec. 1900, p. 42, 143
July–Dec. 1901, p. 36
Jan.–June 1902, p. 67
Jan.–June 1903, pp. 129–34, 178
July–Dec. 1911, pp. 233–52

Revue des Arts Décoratifs, 1900, pp. 336, 337, 338
           1901, pp. 47, 374–375
Kunsthandwerk um 1900, Darmstadt, exhibition catalogue,
    1965, Ill. No. 440
La Lorraine Artiste, 1899, pp. 5–7, 13–22, 60
           1900, pp. 98–100
           1901, pp. 25–30, 33–35, 59–60
           1903, p. 83, 85, 215, 216
           1904, pp. 37–40
Littérature et Beaux-Arts, pp. 621–25
Bulletin des Sociétés Artistiques de l'Est, 1900–1904, pp.
    154–61, 195–207
Revue Lorraine Illustrée, No. 3, 1906, pp. 99, 129
L'Estampille, Feb. 1978, pp. 10–17
Meubles et Décors, No. 809, December 1965, pp. 102–05

GALLEREY, Mathieu
Art et Décoration, Jan.–June 1904, pp. 82–84, 90, 92
           July–Dec. 1905, p. 115
           Jan.–June 1907, p. 17
Art et Industrie (Nancy), 1909, July, p. 19
           1910, p. 87
L'Art Décoratif, Jan.–June 1904, p. 94–96
           July–Dec. 1906, pp. 32, 205–06
           Jan.–June 1907, p. 163

GAUTHIER, Camille
Art et Industrie (Nancy), July 1909, p. 63
           1910, pp. 75–77
La Lorraine Artiste, 1899, p. 34
           1901, p. 54
           1903, p. 133
Art et Décoration, Jan.–June 1898, p. 111
           July–Dec. 1898, p. 11
           Jan.–June 1903, p. 136
Bulletin des Sociétés Artistiques de l'Est, Dec. 1904, p. 22
Meubles et Décors, No. 810, January 1966, Ills. 11, 12
Revue Lorraine Illustrée, No. 3, 1906, p. 132
L'Art Décoratif, Jan.–June 1903, pp. 180–81
           Jan.–June 1905, pp. 100–04

GRUBER, Jacques
Art et Décoration, Jan.–June 1903, pp. 137–38
Meubles et Décors, No. 810, January 1966, pp. 37–38
La Lorraine Illustrée, 1901, pp. 76, 99–100, 101
           1906, pp. 97, 104
L'Estampille, Feb. 1978, p. 16
Bulletin des Sociétés Artistiques de l'Est, Dec. 1904, Ill. 147
La Lorraine Artiste, 1899
L'Art Décoratif, Jan.–June 1903, pp. 176, 180
Art et Industrie (Nancy), Jan. 1911, p. 65.
           July 1909, pp. 64–7

GUIMARD, Hector
Guimard, Horta, Van de Velde, exhibition catalogue,
    Musée des Arts Décoratifs, Paris, 1971
Art Nouveau, Museum of Modern Art, exhibition
    catalogue
Um 1900, Zurich, exhibition catalogue, Ill. No. 13
Revue des Arts Décoratifs, 1900, p. 288
L'Art Décoratif, Jan.–June 1900, pp. 70, 217
Art et Décoration, Jan.–June 1897, p. 106
           Jan.–June 1899, p. 81
           Jan.–June 1904, p. 91

HAMM, Henri
Art et Décoration, Jan.–June 1902, p. 186
L'Art Décoratif, July–Dec. 1903, p. 237
Meubles et Décors, No. 813, April 1966, p. 79

HÉROLD, Louis-Alphonse
Art et Décoration, Jan.–June 1899, pp. 86–87
           Jan.–June 1900, p. 50
           Jan.–June 1901, p. 140
           Jan.–June 1902, p. 180
L'Art Décoratif, Jan.–June 1901, p. 51
           July–Dec. 1902, p. 172
           Jan. 1903, p. 215
           July 1903, p. 66
           July–Dec. 1906, pp. 27, 30

HESTAUX, Louis
Art et Décoration, Jan.–June 1897, p. 77
           Jan.–June 1898, p. 110
           July–Dec. 1898, pp. 16, 17, 21
           July–Dec. 1901, p. 38
           Jan.–June 1903, p. 130
Meubles et Décors, No. 810, January 1966, Ill. No. 10, p. 33
Revue des Arts Décoratifs, 1901, p. 203
Bulletin des Sociétés Artistiques de l'est, No. 12, Dec. 1904,
    p. 221
La Lorraine Artiste, 1899, p. 60
           1901, 1 May 1901, p. 169
           1902, pp. 151–3

HOENTSCHEL, Georges
Art et Décoration, July–Dec. 1900, p. 100
Meubles et Décors, No. 810, January 1966, p. 29

LAMBERT, Théodore
Art et Décoration, Jan.–June 1897, p. 108
           July–Dec. 1901, pp. 34–35
           July–Dec. 1902, pp. 182, 184
           Jan.–June 1904, pp. 89–90
           July–Dec. 1905, p. 118
           Jan.–June 1907, pp. 162–63
           July–Dec. 1907, p. 115
           July–Dec. 1913, pp. 24–25

RAPIN, Henri
Meubles et Décors, No. 813, April 1966, pp. 79, 81

SAUVAGE, Henri
Art et Décoration, Jan.–June 1899, pp. 65–75
    July–Dec. 1899, pp. 42, 46
    Jan.–June 1900, p. 50
    Jan.–June 1901, pp. 129, 132, 135, 136, 196
    July–Dec. 1901, pp. 40, 114
    Jan.–June 1903
    Jan.–June 1904, p. 82
L'Art Décoratif, June 1900, p. 92
    Jan. 1903, pp. 148–52
    July–Dec. 1903, p. 62
    Jan. 1904, pp. 91–92, 96, 216
    July–Dec. 1906, p. 206
Revue des Arts Décoratifs, 1901, pp. 205, 207
Meubles et Décors, No. 814, May 1966, pp. 98–99

SELMERSHEIM, Pierre
Art et Décoration, Jan.–June 1901, p. 199
    Jan.–June 1902, pp. 177–78, 184
    July–Dec. 1913, pp. 30–31
L'Art Décoratif, Jan.–June 1901, pp. 38, 40, 163
    July–Dec. 1902, pp. 381–90
    July–Dec. 1906, pp. 32, 209

Revue des Arts Décoratifs, 1901, p. 207
Meubles et Décors, No. 814, May 1966, Ills. Nos. 6, 7

SOREL, L.
L'Art Décoratif, July–Dec. 1900, p. 68
    Jan.–June 1901, p. 56
    Jan.–June 1904, p. 98
Art et Décoration, Jan.–June 1898, pp. 65–69
    Jan.–June 1901, pp. 131, 138, 194–97
    July–Dec. 1901, pp. 35, 124, 158
Revue des Arts Décoratifs, 1901, p. 211
Meubles et Décors, No. 817, August 1966, pp. 101, 102

VALLIN
Art et Industrie (Nancy), 1909, pp. 52–67
Meubles et Décors, No. 810, January 1966, Ills. No. 7–9
Art et Décoration, Jan.–June 1903, pp. 130, 133, 137
Revue Lorraine Illustrée, 1906, pl. V
La Lorraine, 1902, pp. 276–77, 279–81
    1904 (No. 17 & 18), pp. 260–75
Bulletin des Sociétés Artistiques de l'Est, 1904, pl. 349
La Lorraine Artiste, 1899, pp. 34–39
Revue Lorraine Illustrée, No. 3, 1906, pp. 98–100, 102–03, 130, 138
L'Art Décoratif, Jan.–June 1905, pp. 98–99, 103
Art et Industrie, Jan. 1911
L'Art Décoratif, Jan.–June 1903, pp. 176, 180

Photographic Credits

Index